CHICKEN SOUP FOR THE SOUL

101 Stories To
Open The Heart &
Rekindle The Spirit

Jack Canfield
and
Mark Victor Hansen

Guideposts®
CARMEL • NEW YORK 10512

We would like to acknowledge the following publishers and individuals for permission to reprint the following material. (Note: The stories that were penned anonymously, that are public domain or were written by Jack Canfield or Mark Victor Hansen are not included in this listing.)

On Courage and *Sachi* from *Sacred Journey of the Peaceful Warrior* by Dan Millman ©1991 Dan Millman — Reprinted by permission of the author and H.J. Kramer, Inc., P.O. Box 1082, Tiburon, CA 94920. All rights reserved.

Another Way. Reprinted by permission of The Putnam Publishing Group from *Safe and Alive* by Terry Dobson. ©1982 Terry Dobson.

The Gentlest Need. Reprinted by Fred T. Wilhelms. Reprinted by permission of the author and *Educational Leadership,* 48, 1:51. ©ASCD.

My Declaration of Self-Esteem and *Everybody Has a Dream* reprinted with the express written permission of the AVANTA Network which was founded by Virginia Satir and has inherited rights to all of her intellectual property. For information about copyright materials of Virginia Satir and/or the AVANTA Network contact: Avanta Network, 310 Third Avenue N.E., Ste. 126, Issaquah, WA 98027 or call (206) 391-7310.

Why I Chose My Father To Be My Dad from *The Six Ingredients of Self-Esteem and How They are Developed in Your Children* by Bettie B. Youngs. ©1992 Rawson Assoc.

A Mom's Life from *Funny Sauce* by Delia Ephron. ©1982, 1983, 1986 by Delia Ephron. Used by permission of Viking Penguin, a division of Penguin Books, USA, Inc.

On Parenting from *The Prophet* by Kahlil Gibran. ©1923 by Kahlil Gibran and renewed 1951 by Administrators C.T.A. of Kahlil Gibran Estate and Mary G. Gibran. Reprinted by permission of Alfred A. Knopf, Inc.

Bilding Me A Fewchr. Copyright ©1990, ProTeach Publications. Authored by Frank Trujillo. All rights reserved. (800) 233-3541.

All I Ever Really Needed To Know I Learned in Kindergarten. Reprinted by permission of Villard Books, a division of Random House, Inc. ©1986, 1988 Robert Fulghum.

(Continued on page 304)

This Guideposts edition is published by special arrangement with Health Communications, Inc.

Cover design by Barbara Bergman

If there is light in the soul,
There will be beauty in the person.
If there is beauty in the person,
There will be harmony in the house.
If there is harmony in the house,
There will be order in the nation.
If there is order in the nation,
There will be peace in the world.

Chinese Proverb

With love we dedicate this book to our wives,
Georgia and Patty, and our children,
Christopher, Oran, Kyle, Elizabeth and Melanie,
who are chicken soup for our souls.
You are constantly opening our hearts and
rekindling our spirits. We love you very much!

Acknowledgments

This book took almost two years from conception to completion. It was a labor of love and took the combined efforts of many people. We especially wish to acknowledge the following:

Patty Mitchell, who typed and retyped each of these stories at least five times. Her commitment to this project included many weekdays until 10:00 PM and lots of weekends. Thank you, Patty! We couldn't have done it without you.

Kim Wiele, for the monumental typing and retyping of many of the stories, handling much of the extensive research and coordinating all of the seemingly endless work to secure copyright permission of the stories we didn't write ourselves. She did a terrific job. Thanks, Kim.

Kate Driesen, who assisted with the typing, read and commented on each story and helped with much of the research. You were always there when there were deadlines. Thank you.

Wanda Pate, who contributed endlessly in helping with typing and research.

Cheryl Millikin, who kept the processing and flow of the material working all along.

Lisa Williams, for taking care of Mark's business so he could be dedicated to this book.

Larry Price and Mark Powers, for keeping everything else going while this book was being written.

To the hundreds of people who listened, read and commented on these stories, poems and quotes.

To all of our friends at the National Speakers Association, who so generously gave of their own material to complete this book. We especially want to thank Dottie Walters for her continued encouragement and support.

To Frank Siccone, a dear friend, who contributed several of his stories and quotes.

To Jeff Herman, for being such an inspired literary agent and for believing in the book from the beginning. Jeff, we love working with you.

To Peter Vegso, Gary Seidler and Barbara Nichols at Health Communications for catching the vision of the book long before anyone else did. We appreciate your enthusiastic support.

To Cindy Spitzer, who wrote and edited several of the most important stories in this book. Cindy, your contribution was invaluable.

To Marie Stilkind, our editor at Health Communications, for her timeless efforts in bringing this book to its high state of excellence.

To Bob Proctor, who contributed several stories and anecdotes from his voluminous file of teaching stories. Thank you, Bob. You've been a good friend.

To Brandon Hall, who helped us with two stories.

We also want to thank the following people for giving us very valuable feedback on the first draft: Ellen Angelis, Kim Angelis, Jacob Blass, Rick Canfield, Dan Drubin, Kathy Fellows, Patty Hansen, Norman Howe, Ann Husch, Tomas Nani, Dave Potter, Danielle Lee, Michele Martin, Georgia Noble, Lee Potts, Linda Price, Martin Rutte, Lou Tartaglia, Dottie Walters, Rebecca Weidekehr, Harold C. Wells.

Contents

1. ON LOVE

6. OVERCOMING OBSTACLES

7. ECLECTIC WISDOM

Introduction

We know everything we need to know to end the needless emotional suffering that many people currently experience. High self-esteem and personal effectiveness is available to anyone willing to take the time to pursue it.

It is difficult to translate the spirit of a live presentation into the written word. Stories we tell every day have had to be rewritten five times to work as well in print as they do live. When you are reading these stories, please forget everything you ever learned in your speed-reading classes. Slow down. Listen to the words in your heart as well as in your mind. Savor each story. Let it touch you. Ask yourself, what does it awaken in me? What does it suggest for my life? What feeling or action does it call forth from my inner being? Let yourself have a personal relationship with each story.

Some stories will speak louder to you than others. Some will have deeper meaning. Some will make you cry. Some will make you laugh. Some will give you a warm feeling all over. Some may hit you right between the eyes. There is no right reaction. There is only *your* reaction. Let it happen and let it be.

Don't hurry through this book. Take your time. Enjoy it. Savor it. Engage it with your whole being. It represents thousands of hours of culling the "best of the best" from our 40 years of combined experience.

One last thing: Reading a book like this is a little like sitting down to eat a meal of all desserts. It may be a little too rich. It is a meal with no vegetables, salad or bread. It is all essence with very little froth.

In our seminars and workshops we take more time to set up and discuss the implications of each story. There are more explanations and explorations of how to apply the lessons and principles to your everyday life. Don't just read these stories. Take the time to digest them and make them your own.

If you find yourself moved to share a story with others, do it. When a story makes you think of another person, call the person it brings to mind and share it. Engage these stories and let them move you to do whatever comes up for you. They are meant to inspire and motivate you.

For a lot of these stories we went back to the original source and asked them to write it or tell it in their own words. Many of the stories will be in their voice, not ours. We have attributed every story we could to the original source. For all of those that are from fellow speakers and trainers, we have included a contributors section in the back of the book where we have listed their name, address and phone number so you can contact them yourself if you wish.

We hope you will enjoy reading this book as much as we have enjoyed writing it.

1

ON LOVE

The day will come when, after harnessing space, the winds, the tides and gravitation, we shall harness for God the energies of love. And on that day, for the second time in the history of the world, we shall have discovered fire.

Tielhard de Chardin

Love: The One Creative Force

Spread love everywhere you go: first of all in your own house. Give love to your children, to your wife or husband, to a next door neighbor . . . Let no one ever come to you without leaving better and happier. Be the living expression of God's kindness; kindness in your face, kindness in your eyes, kindness in your smile, kindness in your warm greeting.

Mother Teresa

A college professor had his sociology class go into the Baltimore slums to get case histories of 200 young boys. They were asked to write an evaluation of each boy's future. In every case the students wrote, "He hasn't got a chance." Twenty-five years later another sociology professor came across the earlier study. He had his students follow up on the project to see what had happened to these boys. With the exception of 20 boys who had moved away or died, the students learned that 176 of the remaining 180 had achieved more than ordinary success as lawyers, doctors and businessmen.

The professor was astounded and decided to pursue the matter further. Fortunately, all the men were in the area and he was able to ask each one, "How do you account for your success?" In each case the reply came with feeling, "There was a teacher."

The teacher was still alive, so he sought her out and asked the old but still alert lady what magic formula she had used to pull these boys out of the slums into successful achievement.

The teacher's eyes sparkled and her lips broke into a gentle smile. "It's really very simple," she said. "I loved those boys."

Eric Butterworth

All I Remember

When my father spoke to me, he always began the conversation with "Have I told you yet today how much I adore you?" The expression of love was reciprocated and, in his later years, as his life began to visibly ebb, we grew even closer . . . if that were possible.

At 82 he was ready to die, and I was ready to let him go so that his suffering would end. We laughed and cried and held hands and told each other of our love and agreed that it was time. I said, "Dad, after you've gone I want a sign from you that you're fine." He laughed at the absurdity of that; Dad didn't believe in reincarnation. I wasn't positive I did either, but I had had many experiences that convinced me I could get some signal "from the other side."

My father and I were so deeply connected I felt his heart attack in my chest at the moment he died. Later I mourned that the hospital, in their sterile wisdom, had not let me hold his hand as he had slipped away.

Day after day I prayed to hear from him, but nothing happened. Night after night I asked for a dream before I fell asleep. And yet four long months passed and I heard and felt nothing but grief at his loss. Mother had died five years before of Alzheimer's and, though I had grown daughters of my own, I felt like a lost child.

One day, while I was lying on a massage table in a dark quiet room waiting for my appointment, a wave of longing for my father swept over me. I began to wonder if I had been too demanding in asking for a sign from him. I noticed that my mind was in a hyper-acute state. I experienced an unfamiliar clarity in which I could have added long columns of figures in my head. I checked to make sure I was awake and not dreaming, and I saw that I was as far removed from a dreamy state as one could possibly be. Each thought I had was like a drop of water disturbing a still pond, and I marveled at the peacefulness of each passing moment. Then I thought, "I've been trying to control the messages from the other side; I will stop that now."

Suddenly my mother's face appeared — my mother, as she had been before Alzheimer's disease had stripped her of her mind, her humanity and 50 pounds. Her magnificent silver hair crowned her sweet face. She was so real and so close I felt I could reach out and touch her. She looked as she had a dozen years ago, before the wasting away had begun. I even smelled the fragrance of Joy, her favorite perfume. She seemed to be waiting and did not speak. I wondered how it could happen that I was thinking of my father and my mother appeared, and I felt a little guilty that I had not asked for her as well.

I said, "Oh, Mother, I'm so sorry that you had to suffer with that horrible disease."

She tipped her head slightly to one side, as though to acknowledge what I had said about her suffering. Then she smiled — a beautiful smile — and said very distinctly, "But all I remember is love." And she disappeared.

I began to shiver in a room suddenly gone cold, and I knew in my bones that the love we give and receive is all that matters and all that is remembered. Suffering disappears; love remains.

Her words are the most important I have ever heard, and that moment is forever engraved on my heart.

I have not yet seen or heard from my father, but I have no doubts that someday, when I least expect it, he will appear and say, "Have I told you yet today that I love you?"

Bobbie Probstein

Heart Song

Once upon a time there was a great man who married the woman of his dreams. With their love, they created a little girl. She was a bright and cheerful little girl and the great man loved her very much.

When she was very little, he would pick her up, hum a tune and dance with her around the room, and he would tell her, "I love you, little girl."

When the little girl was growing up, the great man would hug her and tell her, "I love you, little girl." The little girl would pout and say, "I'm not a little girl anymore." Then the man would laugh and say, "But to me, you'll always be my little girl."

The little girl who-was-not-little-anymore left her home and went into the world. As she learned more about herself, she learned more about the man. She saw that he truly was great and strong, for now she recognized his strengths. One of his strengths was his ability to express his love to his family. It didn't matter where she went in the world, the man would call her and say, "I love you, little girl."

The day came when the little girl who-was-not-little-anymore received a phone call. The great man was damaged. He had had a stroke. He was aphasic, they explained to the girl. He couldn't talk anymore and they weren't sure that he could understand the words spoken to him. He could no longer smile, laugh, walk, hug, dance or tell the little girl who-was-not-little-anymore that he loved her.

And so she went to the side of the great man. When she walked into the room and saw him, he looked small and not strong at all. He looked at her and tried to speak, but he could not.

The little girl did the only thing she could do. She climbed up on the bed next to the great man. Tears ran from both of their eyes and she drew her arms around the useless shoulders of her father.

Her head on his chest, she thought of many things. She remembered the wonderful times together and how she had always felt protected and cherished by the great man. She felt grief for the loss she was to endure, the words of love that had comforted her.

And then she heard from within the man, the beat of his heart. The heart where the music and the words had always lived. The heart beat on, steadily unconcerned about the damage to the rest of the body. And while she rested there, the magic happened. She heard what she needed to hear.

His heart beat out the words that his mouth could no longer say . . .

I love you
I love you
I love you
Little girl
Little girl
Little girl

And she was comforted.

Patty Hansen

True Love

Moses Mendelssohn, the grandfather of the well-known German composer, was far from being handsome. Along with a rather short stature, he had a grotesque hunchback.

One day he visited a merchant in Hamburg who had a lovely daughter named Frumtje. Moses fell hopelessly in love with her. But Frumtje was repulsed by his misshapen appearance.

When it came time for him to leave, Moses gathered his courage and climbed the stairs to her room to take one last opportunity to speak with her. She was a vision of heavenly beauty, but caused him deep sadness by her refusal to look at him. After several attempts at conversation, Moses shyly asked, "Do you believe marriages are made in heaven?"

"Yes," she answered, still looking at the floor. "And do you?"

"Yes I do," he replied. "You see, in heaven at the birth of each boy, the Lord announces which girl he will marry. When I was born, my future bride was pointed out to me. Then the Lord added, 'But your wife will be humpbacked.'

"Right then and there I called out, 'Oh Lord, a humpbacked woman would be a tragedy. Please, Lord, give me the hump and let her be beautiful.' "

Then Frumtje looked up into his eyes and was stirred by some deep memory. She reached out and gave Mendelssohn her hand and later became his devoted wife.

Barry and Joyce Vissell

The Hugging Judge

Don't bug me! Hug me!

Bumper Sticker

Lee Shapiro is a retired judge. He is also one of the most genuinely loving people we know. At one point in his career, Lee realized that love is the greatest power there is. As a result, Lee became a hugger. He began offering everybody a hug. His colleagues dubbed him "the hugging judge" (as opposed to the hanging judge, we suppose). The bumper sticker on his car reads, "Don't bug me! Hug me!"

About six years ago Lee created what he calls his *Hugger Kit*. On the outside it reads "A heart for a hug." The inside contains thirty little red embroidered hearts with stickums on the back. Lee will take out his Hugger Kit, go around to people and offer them a little red heart in exchange for a hug.

Lee has become so well known for this that he is often invited to keynote conferences and conventions, where he shares his message of unconditional love. At a conference in San Francisco, the local news media challenged him by saying, "It is easy to give out hugs here in the conference to people who self-selected to be here. But this would never work in the real world."

They challenged Lee to give away some hugs on the streets of San Francisco. Followed by a television crew from the local news station, Lee went out onto the street. First he approached a woman walking by. "Hi, I'm Lee Shapiro, the hugging judge. I'm giving out these hearts in exchange for a hug." "Sure," she replied. "Too easy," challenged the local commentator. Lee looked around. He saw a meter maid who was being given a hard time by the owner of a BMW to whom she was giving a ticket. He marched up to her, camera crew in tow, and said, "You look like you could use a hug. I'm the hugging judge and I'm offering you one." She accepted.

The television commentator threw down one final challenge. "Look, here comes a bus. San Francisco bus drivers are the toughest, crabbiest, meanest people in the whole town. Let's see you get him to hug you." Lee took the challenge.

As the bus pulled up to the curb, Lee said, "Hi, I'm Lee Shapiro, the hugging judge. This has got to be one of the most stressful jobs in the whole world. I'm offering hugs to people today to lighten the load a little. Would you like one?" The six-foot-two, 230-pound bus driver got out of his seat, stepped down and said, "Why not?"

Lee hugged him, gave him a heart and waved goodbye as the bus pulled out. The TV crew was speechless. Finally, the commentator said, "I have to admit, I'm very impressed."

One day Lee's friend Nancy Johnston showed up on his doorstep. Nancy is a professional clown and she was wearing her clown costume, makeup and all. "Lee, grab a bunch of your Hugger Kits and let's go out to the home for the disabled."

When they arrived at the home, they started giving out balloon hats, hearts and hugs to the patients. Lee was uncomfortable. He had never before hugged people who were terminally ill, severely retarded or quadraplegic. It was definitely a stretch. But after a while it became easier with Nancy and Lee acquiring an entourage of doctors, nurses and orderlies who followed them from ward to ward.

After several hours they entered the last ward. These were 34 of the worst cases Lee had seen in his life. The feeling was so grim it took his heart away. But out of their commitment to share their love and to make a difference, Nancy and Lee started working their way around the room followed by the entourage of medical staff, all of whom by now had hearts on their collars and balloon hats on their heads.

Finally, Lee came to the last person, Leonard. Leonard was wearing a big white bib which he was drooling on. Lee looked at Leonard dribbling onto his bib and said, "Let's go, Nancy, there's no way we can get through to this person." Nancy replied, "C'mon, Lee. He's a fellow human being, too, isn't he?" Then she placed a funny balloon hat on his head. Lee took one of his little red hearts and placed it on Leonard's bib. He took a deep breath, leaned down and gave Leonard a hug.

All of a sudden Leonard began to squeal, "Eeeeehh! Eeeeeehh!" Some of the other patients in the room began to clang things together. Lee turned to the staff for some sort of explanation only to find that every doctor, nurse and orderly was crying. Lee asked the head nurse, "What's going on?"

Lee will never forget what she said: "This is the first time in 23 years we've ever seen Leonard smile."

How simple it is to make a difference in the lives of others.

Jack Canfield and Mark V. Hansen

© 1984 United Feature Syndicate, Inc.
5-12
YOU CAN ALWAYS TELL WHEN HE'S BEEN LISTENING TO LEO BUSCAGLIA TAPES..
SCHULZ

It Can't Happen Here?

We need 4 hugs a day for survival. We need 8 hugs a day for maintenance. We need 12 hugs a day for growth.

Virginia Satir

We always teach people to hug each other in our workshops and seminars. Most people respond by saying, "You could never hug people where I work." Are you sure?

Here is a letter from a graduate of one of our seminars.

Dear Jack,

I started out this day in rather a bleak mood. My friend Rosalind stopped over and asked me if I was giving hugs today. I just grumbled something but then I began to think about hugs and everything during the week. I would look at the sheet you gave us on *How to Keep the Seminar Alive* and I would cringe when I got to the part about giving and getting hugs because I couldn't imagine giving hugs to the people at work.

Well, I decided to make it "hugs day" and I started giving hugs to the customers who came to my counter. It was great to see how people just brightened up. An MBA student jumped up on top of the counter and did a dance. Some people actually came back and asked for more. These two Xerox repair guys, who were kind of just walking along not really talking to each other, were so surprised, they just woke up and suddenly were talking and laughing down the hall.

It feels like I hugged everybody in the Wharton Business School, plus whatever was wrong with me this morning, which included some physical pain, is all gone. I'm sorry that this letter is so long but I'm just really excited. The neatest thing was, at one point there were about 10 people all hugging each other out in front of my counter. I couldn't believe this was happening.

Love,
Pamela Rogers

P.S.: On the way home I hugged a policeman on 37th Street. He said, "Wow! Policemen never get hugs. Are you sure you don't want to throw something at me?"

Another seminar graduate sent us the following piece on hugging:

Hugging is healthy. It helps the body's immune system, it keeps you healthier, it cures depression, it reduces stress, it induces sleep, it's invigorating, it's rejuvenating, it has no unpleasant side effects, and hugging is nothing less than a miracle drug.

Hugging is all natural. It is organic, naturally sweet, no pesticides, no preservatives, no artificial ingredients and 100 percent wholesome.

Hugging is practically perfect. There are no movable parts, no batteries to wear out, no periodic check-ups, low energy consumption, high energy yield, inflation proof, nonfattening, no monthly payments, no insurance requirements, theft-proof, nontaxable, nonpolluting and, of course, fully returnable.

Source Unknown

Jack Canfield

Who You Are Makes A Difference

A teacher in New York decided to honor each of her seniors in high school by telling them the difference they each made. Using a process developed by Helice Bridges of Del Mar, California, she called each student to the front of the class, one at a time. First she told them how the student made a difference to her and the class. Then she presented each of them with a blue ribbon imprinted with gold letters which read, "Who I Am Makes a Difference."

Afterwards the teacher decided to do a class project to see what kind of impact recognition would have on a community. She gave each of the students three more ribbons and instructed them to go out and spread this acknowledgment ceremony. Then they were to follow up on the results, see who honored whom and report back to the class in about a week.

One of the boys in the class went to a junior executive in a nearby company and honored him for helping him with his career planning. He gave him a blue ribbon and put it on his shirt. Then he gave him two extra ribbons, and said, "We're doing a class project on recognition, and we'd like you to go out, find somebody to honor, give them a blue ribbon, then give them the extra blue ribbon so they can acknowledge a third person to keep this acknowledgment ceremony going. Then please report back to me and tell me what happened."

Later that day the junior executive went in to see his boss, who had been noted, by the way, as being kind of a grouchy fellow. He sat his boss down and he told him that he deeply admired him for being a creative genius. The boss seemed very surprised. The junior executive asked him if he would accept the gift of the blue ribbon and would he give him permission to put it on him. His surprised boss said, "Well, sure."

The junior executive took the blue ribbon and placed it right on his boss's jacket above his heart. As he gave him the last extra ribbon, he said, "Would you do me a favor? Would you take this extra ribbon and pass it on by honoring somebody else? The young boy who first gave me the ribbons is doing a project in school and we want to keep this recognition ceremony going and find out how it affects people."

That night the boss came home to his 14-year-old son and sat him down. He said, "The most incredible thing happened to me today. I was in my office and one of the junior executives came in and told me he admired me and gave me a blue ribbon for being a creative genius. Imagine. He thinks I'm a creative genius. Then he put this blue ribbon that says 'Who I Am Makes A Difference' on my jacket above my heart. He gave me an extra ribbon and asked me to find somebody else to honor. As I was driving home tonight, I started thinking about whom I would honor with this ribbon and I thought about you. I want to honor you.

"My days are really hectic and when I come home I don't pay a lot of attention to you. Sometimes I scream at you for not getting good enough grades in school and for your bedroom being a mess, but somehow tonight, I just wanted to sit here and, well, just let you know that you do make a difference to me. Besides your mother, you are the most important person in my life. You're a great kid and I love you!"

The startled boy started to sob and sob, and he couldn't stop crying. His whole body shook. He looked up at his father and said through his tears, "I was planning on committing suicide tomorrow, Dad, because I didn't think you loved me. Now I don't need to."

Helice Bridges

One At A Time

A friend of ours was walking down a deserted Mexican beach at sunset. As he walked along, he began to see another man in the distance. As he grew nearer, he noticed that the local native kept leaning down, picking something up and throwing it out into the water. Time and again he kept hurling things out into the ocean.

As our friend approached even closer, he noticed that the man was picking up starfish that had been washed up on the beach and, one at a time, he was throwing them back into the water.

Our friend was puzzled. He approached the man and said, "Good evening, friend. I was wondering what you are doing."

"I'm throwing these starfish back into the ocean. You see, it's low tide right now and all of these starfish have been washed up onto the shore. If I don't throw them back into the sea, they'll die up here from lack of oxygen."

"I understand," my friend replied, "but there must be thousands of starfish on this beach. You can't possibly get to all of them. There are simply too many. And don't you realize this is probably happening on hundreds of beaches all up and down this coast. Can't you see that you can't possibly make a difference?"

The local native smiled, bent down and picked up yet another starfish, and as he threw it back into the sea, he replied, "Made a difference to that one!"

Jack Canfield and Mark V. Hansen

The Gift

Bennet Cerf relates this touching story about a bus that was bumping along a back road in the South.

In one seat a wispy old man sat holding a bunch of fresh flowers. Across the aisle was a young girl whose eyes came back again and again to the man's flowers. The time came for the old man to get off. Impulsively he thrust the flowers into the girl's lap. "I can see you love the flowers," he explained, "and I think my wife would like for you to have them. I'll tell her I gave them to you." The girl accepted the flowers, then watched the old man get off the bus and walk through the gate of a small cemetery.

A Brother Like That

A friend of mine named Paul received an automobile from his brother as a Christmas present. On Christmas Eve when Paul came out of his office, a street urchin was walking around the shiny new car, admiring it. "Is this your car, Mister?" he asked.

Paul nodded. "My brother gave it to me for Christmas." The boy was astounded. "You mean your brother gave it to you and it didn't cost you nothing? Boy, I wish . . ." He hesitated.

Of course Paul knew what he was going to wish for. He was going to wish he had a brother like that. But what the lad said jarred Paul all the way down to his heels.

"I wish," the boy went on, "that I could be a brother like that."

Paul looked at the boy in astonishment, then impulsively he added, "Would you like to take a ride in my automobile?"

"Oh yes, I'd love that."

After a short ride, the boy turned and with his eyes aglow, said, "Mister, would you mind driving in front of my house?"

Paul smiled a little. He thought he knew what the lad wanted. He wanted to show his neighbors that he could ride home in a big automobile. But Paul was wrong again. "Will you stop where those two steps are?" the boy asked.

He ran up the steps. Then in a little while Paul heard him coming back, but he was not coming fast. He was carrying his little crippled brother. He sat him down on the bottom step, then sort of squeezed up against him and pointed to the car.

"There she is, Buddy, just like I told you upstairs. His brother gave it to him for Christmas and it didn't cost him a cent. And some day I'm gonna give you one just like it . . . then you can see for yourself all the pretty things in the Christmas windows that I've been trying to tell you about."

Paul got out and lifted the lad to the front seat of his car. The shining-eyed older brother climbed in beside him and the three of them began a memorable holiday ride.

That Christmas Eve, Paul learned what Jesus meant when he had said: *"It is more blessed to give . . ."*

Dan Clark

On Courage

"So you think I'm courageous?" she asked.

"Yes, I do."

"Perhaps I am. But that's because I've had some inspiring teachers. I'll tell you about one of them. Many years ago, when I worked as a volunteer at Stanford Hospital, I got to know a little girl named Liza who was suffering from a rare and serious disease. Her only chance of recovery appeared to be a blood transfusion from her five-year-old brother, who had miraculously survived the same disease and had developed the antibodies needed to combat the illness. The doctor explained the situation to her little brother, and asked the boy if he would be willing to give his blood to his sister. I saw him hesitate for only a moment before taking a deep breath and saying, 'Yes, I'll do it if it will save Liza.'

"As the transfusion progressed, he lay in a bed next to his sister and smiled, as we all did, seeing the color returning to her cheeks. Then his face grew pale and his smile faded. He looked up at the doctor and asked with a trembling voice, 'Will I start to die right away?'

"Being young, the boy had misunderstood the doctor; he thought he was going to have to give her *all* his blood.

"Yes, I've learned courage," she added, "because I've had inspiring teachers."

Dan Millman

Big Ed

When I arrived in the city to present a seminar on Tough-Minded Management, a small group of people took me to dinner to brief me on the people I would talk to the next day.

The obvious leader of the group was Big Ed, a large burly man with a deep rumbling voice. At dinner he informed me that he was a troubleshooter for a huge international organization. His job was to go into certain divisions or subsidiaries to terminate the employment of the executive in charge.

"Joe," he said, "I'm really looking forward to tomorrow because all of the guys need to listen to a tough guy like you. They're gonna find out that my style is the right one." He grinned and winked.

I smiled. I knew the next day was going to be different from what he was anticipating.

The next day he sat impassively all through the seminar and left at the end without saying anything to me.

Three years later I returned to that city to present another management seminar to approximately the same group. Big Ed was there again. At about ten o'clock he suddenly stood up and asked loudly, "Joe, can I say something to these people?"

I grinned and said, "Sure. When anybody is as big as you are, Ed, he can say anything he wants."

Big Ed went on to say, "All of you guys know me and some of you know what's happened to me. I want to share it, however, with all of you. Joe, I think you'll appreciate it by the time I've finished.

"When I heard you suggest that each of us, in order to become really tough-minded, needed to learn to tell those closest to us that we really loved them, I thought it was a bunch of sentimental garbage. I wondered what in the world that had to do with being tough. You had said toughness is like leather, and hardness is like granite, that the tough mind is open, resilient, disciplined and tenacious. But I couldn't see what love had to do with it.

"That night, as I sat across the living room from my wife, your words were still bugging me. What kind of courage would it take to tell my wife I loved her? Couldn't anybody do it? You had also said this should be in the daylight and not in the bedroom. I found myself clearing my throat and starting and then stopping. My wife looked up and asked me what I had said, and I answered, 'Oh nothing.' Then suddenly, I got up, walked across the room, nervously pushed her newspaper aside and said, 'Alice, I love you.' For a minute she looked startled. Then the tears came to her eyes and she said softly, 'Ed, I love you, too, but this is the first time in 25 years you've said it like that.'

"We talked a while about how love, if there's enough of it, can dissolve all kinds of tensions, and suddenly I decided on the spur of the moment to call my oldest son in New York. We have never really communicated well. When I got him on the phone, I blurted out, 'Son, you're liable to think I'm drunk, but I'm not. I just thought I'd call you and tell you I love you.'

"There was a pause at his end and then I heard him say quietly, 'Dad, I guess I've known that, but it's sure good to hear. I want you to know I love you, too.' We had a good chat and then I called my youngest son in San Francisco. We had been closer. I told him the same thing and this, too, led to a real fine talk like we'd never really had.

"As I lay in bed that night thinking, I realized that all the things you'd talked about that day — real management nuts and bolts — took on extra meaning, and I could get a handle on how to apply them if I really understood and practiced tough-minded love.

"I began to read books on the subject. Sure enough, Joe, a lot of great people had a lot to say, and I began to realize the enormous practicality of applied love in my life, both at home and at work.

"As some of you guys here know, I really changed the way I work with people. I began to listen more and to really hear. I learned what it was like to try to get to know people's strengths rather than dwelling on their weaknesses. I began to discover the real pleasure of helping build their confidence. Maybe the most important thing of all was that I really began to understand that an excellent way to show love and respect for people was to expect them to use their strengths to meet objectives we had worked out together.

"Joe, this is my way of saying thanks. Incidentally, talk about practical! I'm now executive vice-president of the company and they call me a pivotal leader. Okay, you guys, now listen to this guy!"

Joe Batten

Love And The Cabbie

I was in New York the other day and rode with a friend in a taxi. When we got out, my friend said to the driver, "Thank you for the ride. You did a superb job of driving."

The taxi driver was stunned for a second. Then he said, "Are you a wise guy or something?"

"No, my dear man, and I'm not putting you on. I admire the way you keep cool in heavy traffic."

"Yeah," the driver said and drove off.

"What was that all about?" I asked.

"I am trying to bring love back to New York," he said. "I believe it's the only thing that can save the city."

"How can one man save New York?"

"It's not one man. I believe I have made that taxi driver's day. Suppose he has 20 fares. He's going to be nice to those 20 fares because someone was nice to him. Those fares in turn will be kinder to their employees or shopkeepers or waiters or even their own families. Eventually the goodwill could spread to at least 1,000 people. Now that isn't bad, is it?"

"But you're depending on that taxi driver to pass your goodwill to others."

"I'm not depending on it," my friend said. "I'm aware that the system isn't foolproof so I might deal with ten different people today. If out of ten I can make three happy, then eventually I can indirectly influence the attitudes of 3,000 more."

"It sounds good on paper," I admitted, "but I'm not sure it works in practice."

"Nothing is lost if it doesn't. It didn't take any of my time to tell that man he was doing a good job. He neither received a larger tip nor a smaller tip. If it fell on deaf ears, so what? Tomorrow there will be another taxi driver I can try to make happy."

"You're some kind of a nut," I said.

"That shows how cynical you have become. I have made a study of this. The thing that seems to be lacking, besides money of course, for our postal employees, is that no one tells people who work for the post office what a good job they're doing."

"But they're not doing a good job."

"They're not doing a good job because they feel no one cares if they do or not. Why shouldn't someone say a kind word to them?"

We were walking past a structure in the process of being built and passed five workmen eating their lunch. My friend stopped. "That's a magnificent job you men have done. It must be difficult and dangerous work."

The workmen eyed my friend suspiciously.

"When will it be finished?"

"June," a man grunted.

"Ah. That really is impressive. You must all be very proud."

We walked away. I said to him, "I haven't seen anyone like you since *The Man From LaMancha*."

"When those men digest my words, they will feel better for it. Somehow the city will benefit from their happiness."

"But you can't do this all alone!" I protested. "You're just one man."

"The most important thing is not to get discouraged. Making people in the city become kind again is not an easy job, but if I can enlist other people in my campaign . . ."

"You just winked at a very plain-looking woman," I said.

"Yes, I know," he replied. "And if she's a schoolteacher, her class will be in for a fantastic day."

Art Buchwald

A Simple Gesture

Everybody can be great . . . because anybody can serve. You don't have to have a college degree to serve. You don't have to make your subject and verb agree to serve. You only need a heart full of grace. A soul generated by love.

Martin Luther King, Jr.

Mark was walking home from school one day when he noticed the boy ahead of him had tripped and dropped all of the books he was carrying, along with two sweaters, a baseball bat, a glove and a small tape recorder. Mark knelt down and helped the boy pick up the scattered articles. Since they were going the same way, he helped to carry part of the burden. As they walked Mark discovered the boy's name was Bill, that he loved video games, baseball and history, that he was having a lot of trouble with his other subjects and that he had just broken up with his girlfriend.

They arrived at Bill's home first and Mark was invited in for a Coke and to watch some television. The afternoon passed pleasantly with a few laughs and some shared small talk, then Mark went home. They continued to see each other around school, had lunch together once or twice, then both graduated from junior high school. They ended up in the same high school where they had brief contacts over the years. Finally the long awaited senior year came, and three weeks before graduation, Bill asked Mark if they could talk.

Bill reminded him of the day years ago when they had first met. "Do you ever wonder why I was carrying so many things home that day?" asked Bill. "You see, I cleaned out my locker because I didn't want to leave a mess for anyone else. I had stored away some of my mother's sleeping pills and I was going home to commit suicide. But after we spent some time together talking and laughing, I realized that if I had killed myself, I would have missed that time and so many others that might follow. So you see, Mark, when you picked up my books that day, you did a lot more. You saved my life."

John W. Schlatter

The Smile

Smile at each other, smile at your wife, smile at your husband, smile at your children, smile at each other — it doesn't matter who it is — and that will help you to grow up in greater love for each other.

Mother Teresa

Many Americans are familiar with *The Little Prince,* a wonderful book by Antoine de Saint-Exupery. This is a whimsical and fabulous book and works as a children's story as well as a thought-provoking adult fable. Far fewer are aware of Saint-Exupery's other writings, novels and short stories.

Saint-Exupery was a fighter pilot who fought against the Nazis and was killed in action. Before World War II, he fought in the Spanish Civil War against the fascists. He wrote a fascinating story based on that experience entitled *The Smile (Le Sourire).* It is this story which I'd like to share with you now. It isn't clear whether or not he meant this to be autobiographical or fiction. I choose to believe it to be the former.

He said that he was captured by the enemy and thrown into a jail cell. He was sure that from the contemptuous looks and rough treatment he received from his jailers he would be executed the next day. From here, I'll tell the story as I remember it in my own words.

"I was sure that I was to be killed. I became terribly nervous and distraught. I fumbled in my pockets to see if there were any cigarettes which had escaped their search. I found one and because of my shaking hands, I could barely get it to my lips. But I had no matches, they had taken those.

"I looked through the bars at my jailer. He did not make eye contact with me. After all, one does not make eye contact with a thing, a corpse. I called out to him 'Have you got a light, *por favor*?' He looked at me, shrugged and came over to light my cigarette.

"As he came close and lit the match, his eyes inadvertently locked with mine. At that moment, I smiled. I don't know why I did that. Perhaps it was nervousness, perhaps it was because, when you get very close, one to another, it is very hard not to smile. In any case, I smiled. In that instant, it was as though a spark jumped across the gap between our two hearts, our two human souls. I know he didn't want to, but my smile leaped through the bars and generated a smile on his lips, too. He lit my cigarette but stayed near, looking at me directly in the eyes and continuing to smile.

"I kept smiling at him, now aware of him as a person and not just a jailer. And his looking at me seemed to have a new dimension, too. 'Do you have kids?' he asked.

" 'Yes, here, here.' I took out my wallet and nervously fumbled for the pictures of my family. He, too, took out the pictures of his *ninos* and began to talk about his plans and hopes for them. My eyes filled with tears. I said that I feared that I'd never see my family again, never have the chance to see them grow up. Tears came to his eyes, too.

"Suddenly, without another word, he unlocked my cell and silently led me out. Out of the jail, quietly and by back routes, out of the town. There, at the edge of town, he released me. And without another word, he turned back toward the town.

"My life was saved by a smile."

Yes, the smile — the unaffected, unplanned, natural connection between people. I tell this story in my work because I'd like people to consider that underneath all the layers we construct to protect ourselves, our dignity, our titles, our degrees, our status and our need to be seen in certain ways — underneath all that, remains the authentic, essential self. I'm not afraid to call it *the soul.* I really believe that if that part of you and that part of me could recognize each other, we wouldn't be enemies. We couldn't have hate or envy or fear. I sadly conclude that all those other layers, which we so carefully construct through our lives, distance and insulate us from truly contacting others. Saint-Exupery's story speaks of that magic moment when two souls recognize each other.

I've had just a few moments like that. Falling in love is one example. And looking at a baby. Why do we smile when we see a baby? Perhaps it's because we see someone without all the defensive layers, someone whose smile for us we know to be fully genuine and without guile. And that baby-soul inside us smiles wistfully in recognition.

Hanoch McCarty

Amy Graham

After flying all night from Washington, D.C., I was tired as I arrived at the Mile High Church in Denver to conduct three services and hold a workshop on prosperity consciousness. As I entered the church, Dr. Fred Vogt asked me, "Do you know about the *Make a Wish Foundation?*"

"Yes," I replied.

"Well, Amy Graham has been diagnosed as having terminal leukemia. They gave her three days. Her dying wish was to attend your services."

I was shocked. I felt a combination of elation, awe and doubt. I couldn't believe it. I thought kids who were dying would want to go see Disneyland, meet Sylvester Stallone, Mr. "T" or Arnold Schwartzenneger. Surely they wouldn't want to spend their final days listening to Mark Victor Hansen. Why would a kid with only a few days to live want to come hear a motivational speaker. Suddenly my thoughts were interrupted . . .

"Here's Amy," Vogt said as he put her frail hand in mine. Before me stood a 17-year-old girl wearing a bright red and orange turban to cover her head, which was bald from all of the chemotherapy treatments. Her frail body was bent and weak. She said, "My two goals were to graduate from high school and to attend your sermon. My doctors didn't believe I could do either. They didn't think I'd have enough energy. I got discharged into my parents' care . . . This is my mom and dad."

Tears welled in my eyes; I was choked up. My equilibrium was being shaken. I was totally moved. I cleared my throat, smiled and said, "You and your folks are our guests. Thanks for wanting to come." We hugged, dabbed our eyes and separated.

I've attended many healing seminars in the United States, Canada, Malaysia, New Zealand and Australia. I've watched the best healers at work and I've studied, researched, listened, pondered and questioned what worked, why and how.

That Sunday afternoon I held a seminar that Amy and her parents attended. The audience was packed to overflowing with over a thousand attendees eager to learn, grow and become more fully human.

I humbly asked the audience if they wanted to learn a healing process that might serve them for life. From the stage it appeared that everyone's hand was raised high in the air. They unanimously wanted to learn.

I taught the audience how to vigorously rub their hands together, separate them by two inches and feel the healing energy. Then I paired them off with a partner to feel the healing energy emanating from themselves to another. I said, "If you need a healing, accept one here and now."

The audience was in alignment and it was an ecstatic feeling. I explained that everyone has healing energy and healing potential. Five percent of us have it so dramatically pouring forth from our hands that we could make it our profession. I said, "This morning I was introduced to Amy Graham, a 17-year-old, whose final wish was to be at this seminar. I want to bring her up here and let you all send healing life-force energy toward her. Perhaps we can help. She did not request it. I am just doing this spontaneously because it feels right."

The audience chanted, "Yes! Yes! Yes! Yes!"

Amy's dad led her up onto the stage. She looked frail from all of the chemotherapy, too much bed rest and an absolute lack of exercise. (The doctors hadn't let her walk for the two weeks prior to this seminar.)

I had the group warm up their hands and send her healing energy, after which they gave her a tearful standing ovation.

Two weeks later she called to say that her doctor had discharged her after a total remission. Two years later she called to say she was married.

I have learned never to underestimate the healing power we all have. It is always there to be used for the highest good. We just have to remember to use it.

Mark V. Hansen

A Story For Valentine's Day

Larry and Jo Ann were an ordinary couple. They lived in an ordinary house on an ordinary street. Like any other ordinary couple, they struggled to make ends meet and to do the right things for their children.

They were ordinary in yet another way — they had their squabbles. Much of their conversation concerned what was wrong in their marriage and who was to blame.

Until one day when a most extraordinary event took place.

"You know, Jo Ann, I've got a magic chest of drawers. Every time I open them, they're full of socks and underwear," Larry said. "I want to thank you for filling them all these years."

Jo Ann stared at her husband over the top of her glasses. "What do you want, Larry?"

"Nothing. I just want you to know I appreciate those magic drawers."

This wasn't the first time Larry had done something odd, so Jo Ann pushed the incident out of her mind until a few days later.

"Jo Ann, thank you for recording so many correct check numbers in the ledger this month. You put down the right numbers 15 out of 16 times. That's a record."

Disbelieving what she had heard, Jo Ann looked up from her mending. "Larry, you're always complaining about my recording the wrong check numbers. Why stop now?"

"No reason. I just wanted you to know I appreciate the effort you're making."

Jo Ann shook her head and went back to her mending. "What's got into him?" she mumbled to herself.

Nevertheless, the next day when Jo Ann wrote a check at the grocery store, she glanced at her checkbook to confirm that she had put down the right check number. "Why do I suddenly care about those dumb check numbers?" she asked herself.

She tried to disregard the incident, but Larry's strange behavior intensified.

"Jo Ann, that was a great dinner," he said one evening. "I appreciate all your effort. Why, in the past 15 years I'll bet you've fixed over 14,000 meals for me and the kids."

Then "Gee, Jo Ann, the house looks spiffy. You've really worked hard to get it looking so good." And even "Thanks, Jo Ann, for just being you. I really enjoy your company."

Jo Ann was growing worried. "Where's the sarcasm, the criticism?" she wondered.

Her fears that something peculiar was happening to her husband were confirmed by 16-year-old Shelly, who complained, "Dad's gone bonkers, Mom. He just told me I looked nice. With all this makeup and these sloppy clothes, he still said it. That's not Dad, Mom. What's wrong with him?"

Whatever was wrong, Larry didn't get over it. Day in and day out he continued focusing on the positive.

Over the weeks, Jo Ann grew more accustomed to her mate's unusual behavior and occasionally even gave him a grudging "Thank you." She prided herself on taking it all in stride, until one day something so peculiar happened, she became completely discombobulated:

"I want you to take a break," Larry said. "I am going to do the dishes. So please take your hands off that frying pan and leave the kitchen."

(Long, long pause.) "Thank you, Larry. Thank you very much!"

Jo Ann's step was now a little lighter, her self-confidence higher and once in a while she hummed. She didn't seem to have as many blue moods anymore. "I rather like Larry's new behavior," she thought.

That would be the end of the story except one day another most extraordinary event took place. This time it was Jo Ann who spoke.

"Larry," she said, "I want to thank you for going to work and providing for us all these years. I don't think I've ever told you how much I appreciate it."

Larry has never revealed the reason for his dramatic change of behavior no matter how hard Jo Ann has pushed for an answer, and so it will likely remain one of life's mysteries. But it's one I'm thankful to live with.

You see, I am Jo Ann.

Jo Ann Larsen
Desert News

Carpe Diem!

One who stands as a shining example of courageous expression is John Keating, the transformative teacher portrayed by Robin Williams in *Dead Poets Society*. In this masterful motion picture, Keating takes a group of regimented, uptight and spiritually impotent students at a rigid boarding school and inspires them to make their lives extraordinary.

These young men, as Keating points out to them, have lost sight of their dreams and ambitions. They are automatically living out their parents' programs and expectations for them. They plan to become doctors, lawyers and bankers because that is what their parents have told them they are going to do. But these dry fellows have given hardly any thought to what their hearts are calling them to express.

An early scene in the movie shows Mr. Keating taking the boys down to the school lobby where a trophy case displays photos of earlier graduating classes. "Look at these pictures, boys," Keating tells the students. "The young men you behold had the same fire in their eyes that you do. They planned to take the world by storm and make something magnificent of their lives. That was 70 years ago. Now they are all pushing up daisies. How many of them really lived out their dreams? Did they do what they set out to accomplish?" Then Mr. Keating leans into the cluster of preppies and whispers audibly, *"Carpe diem!* Seize the day!"

At first the students do not know what to make of this strange teacher. But soon they ponder the importance of his words. They come to respect and revere Mr. Keating, who has given them a new vision — or returned their original ones.

> *All of us are walking around with some kind of birthday card we would like to give — some personal expression of joy, creativity or aliveness that we are hiding under our shirt.*

One character in the movie, Knox Overstreet, has a terminal crush on a gorgeous girl. The only problem is that she is the girlfriend of a famous jock. Knox is infatuated with this lovely creature down to a cellular level but he lacks the confidence to approach her. Then he remembers Mr. Keating's advice: *Seize the day!* Knox realizes he cannot just go on dreaming — if he wants her, he is going to have to do something about it. And so he does. Boldly and poetically he declares to her his most sensitive feelings. In the process he gets turned away by her, punched in the nose by her boyfriend and faces embarrassing setbacks. But Knox is unwilling to forsake his dream, so he pursues his heart's desire. Ultimately she feels the genuineness of his caring and opens her heart to him. Although Knox is not especially good-looking or popular, the girl is won over by the power of his sincere intention. He has made his life extraordinary.

I had a chance to practice seizing the day myself. I developed a crush on a cute girl I met in a pet store. She was younger than I, she led a very different lifestyle and we did not have a great deal to talk about. But somehow none of this seemed to matter. I enjoyed being with her and I felt a sparkle in her presence. And it seemed to me she enjoyed my company as well.

When I learned her birthday was coming up, I decided to ask her out. On the threshold of calling her, I sat and looked at the phone for about half an hour. Then I dialed and hung up before it rang. I felt like a high school boy, bouncing between excited anticipation and fear of rejection. A voice from hell kept telling me that she would not like me and that I had a lot of nerve asking her out. But I felt too enthusiastic about being with her to let those fears stop me. Finally I got up the nerve to ask her. She thanked me for asking and told me she already had plans.

I felt shot down. The same voice that told me not to call advised me to give up before I was further embarrassed. But I was intent on seeing what this attraction was about. There was more inside of me that wanted to come to life. I had feelings for this woman, and I had to express them.

I went to the mall and got her a pretty birthday card on which I wrote a poetic note. I walked around the corner to the pet shop where I knew she was working. As I approached the door, that same disturbing voice cautioned me, "What if she doesn't like you? What if she rejects you?" Feeling vulnerable, I stuffed the card under my shirt. I decided that if she showed me signs of affection, I would give it to her; if she was cool to me, I would leave the card hidden. This way I would not be at risk and would avoid rejection or embarrassment.

We talked for a while and I did not get any signs one way or the other from her. Feeling ill-at-ease, I began to make my exit.

As I approached the door, however, another voice spoke to me. It came in a whisper, not unlike that of Mr. Keating. It prompted me, "Remember Knox Overstreet . . . *Carpe Diem!*" Here I was confronted with my aspiration to fully express my heart and my resistance to face the insecurity of emotional nakedness. How can I go around telling other people to live their vision, I asked myself, when I am not living my own? Besides, what's the worst thing that could happen? Any woman would be delighted to receive a poetic birthday card. I decided to seize the day. As I made that choice I felt a surge of courage course through my veins. There was indeed power in intention.

I felt more satisfied and at peace with myself than I had in a long time . . . I needed to learn to open my heart and give love without requiring anything in return.

I took the card out from under my shirt, turned around, walked up to the counter and gave it to her. As I handed it to her I felt an incredible aliveness and excitement — plus fear. (Fritz Perls said that fear is "excitement without breath.") But I did it.

And do you know what? She was not particularly impressed. She said, "Thanks" and put the card aside without even opening it. My heart sank. I felt disappointed and rejected. Getting no response seemed even worse than a direct brush-off.

I offered a polite good-bye and walked out of the store. Then something amazing happened. I began to feel exhilarated. A huge rush of internal satisfaction welled up within me and surged through my whole being. I had expressed my heart and that felt fantastic! I had stretched beyond fear and gone out on the dance floor. Yes, I had been a little clumsy, but I did it. (Emmet Fox said, "Do it trembling if you must, but do it!") I had put my heart on the line without demanding a guarantee of the results. I did not give in order to get something back. I opened my feelings to her without an attachment to a particular response.

> *The dynamics that are required to make any relationship work: Just keep putting your love out there.*

My exhilaration deepened to a warm bliss. I felt more satisfied and at peace with myself than I had in a long time. I realized the purpose of the whole experience: I needed to learn to open my heart and give love without requiring anything in return. This experience was not about creating a relationship with this woman. It was about deepening my relationship with myself. And I did it. Mr. Keating would have been proud. But most of all, I was proud.

I have not seen the girl much since then, but that experience changed my life. Through that simple interaction I clearly saw the dynamics that are required to make any relationship and perhaps the whole world work: *Just keep putting your love out there.*

We believe that we are hurt when we don't receive love. But that is not what hurts us. Our pain comes when we do not *give* love. We were born to love. You might say that we are divinely created love machines. We function most powerfully when we are giving love. The world has led us to believe that our well-being is dependent on other people loving us. But this is the kind of upside-down thinking that has caused so many of our problems. The truth is that our well-being is dependent on our *giving* love. It is not about what comes back; it is about *what goes out!*

Alan Cohen

I Know You, You're Just Like Me!

One of our closest friends is Stan Dale. Stan teaches a seminar on love and relationships called Sex, Love and Intimacy. Several years ago, in an effort to learn what the people in the Soviet Union were really like, he took 29 people to the Soviet Union for two weeks. When he wrote about his experiences in his newsletter, we were deeply touched by the following anecdote.

While walking through a park in the industrial city of Kharkov, I spotted an old Russian veteran of World War II. They are easily identified by the medals and ribbons they still proudly display on their shirts and jackets. This is not an act of egotism. It is their country's way of honoring those who helped save Russia, even though 20 million Russians were killed by the Nazis. I went up to this old man sitting with his wife and said, "Droozhba, emir" (friendship and peace). The man looking at me as if in disbelief, took the button we had made for the trip that said "Friendship" in Russian and showed a map of the U.S. and the U.S.S.R. being held by loving hands, and said, "Americanski?" I replied, "Da, Americanski. Droozhba, emir." He clasped both my hands as if we were long lost brothers and repeated again, "Americanski!" This time there was recognition and love in his statement.

For the next few minutes he and his wife spoke in Russian as if I understood every word, and I spoke English as if I knew he would understand. You know what? Neither of us understood a word, but we surely understood each other. We hugged, and laughed and cried, all the while saying, "Droozhba, emir, Americanski." "I love you, I am proud to be in your country, we do not want war. *I love you!*"

After about five minutes we said good-bye, and the seven of us in our little group walked on. About 15 minutes later, some considerable distance on, this same old veteran caught up with us. He came up to me, took off his Order of Lenin medal (probably his most prized possession) and pinned it to my jacket. He then kissed me on the lips and gave me one of the warmest, most loving hugs I have ever received. Then we both cried, looked into each other's eyes for the longest time, and said, "Dossvedanya" (good-bye).

The above story is symbolic of our entire "Citizen Diplomacy" trip to the Soviet Union. Every day we met and touched hundreds of people in every possible and impossible setting. Neither the Russians nor ourselves will ever be the same. There are now hundreds of school children from the three schools we visited who will not be quite so ready to think of Americans as people who want to "nuke" them. We danced, sang and played with children of every age, and then we hugged, kissed and shared presents. They gave us flowers, cakes, buttons, paintings, dolls, but most importantly, their hearts and open minds.

More than once we were invited to be members of wedding parties, and no biological family member could have been more warmly accepted, greeted and feted than we were. We hugged, kissed, danced and drank champagne, schnapps and vodka with the bride and groom, as well as Momma and Poppa and the rest of the family.

In Kursk, we were hosted by seven Russian families who volunteered to take us in for a wonderful evening of food, drink and conversation. Four hours later, none of us wanted to part. Our group now has a complete new family in Russia.

The following night "our family" was feted by us at our hotel. The band played until almost midnight, and guess what? Once again we ate, drank, talked, danced and cried when it came time to say good-bye. We danced every dance as if we were passionate lovers, which is exactly what we were.

I could go on forever about our experiences, and yet there would be no way to convey to you exactly how we felt. How would you feel when you arrived at your hotel in Moscow, if there were a telephone message waiting for you, written in Russian, from Mikhail Gorbachev's office saying he regretted he could not meet with you that weekend because he would be out of town, but instead he had arranged for your entire group to meet for two hours in a round-table discussion with about a half-dozen members of the Central Committee? We had an extremely frank discussion about everything, including sex.

How would you feel if more than a dozen old ladies, wearing babushkas, came down from the steps of their apartment buildings and hugged and kissed you? How would you feel when your guides, Tanya and Natasha, told you and the whole group that they had never seen anyone like you? And when we left, all 30 of us cried because we had fallen in love with these fabulous women, and they with us. Yes, how would you feel? Probably just like us.

Each of us had our own experience, of course, but the collective experience bears out one thing for certain: The only way we are ever going to ensure peace on this planet is to adopt the entire world as "our family." We are going to have to hug them, and kiss them. And dance and play with them. And we are going to have to sit and talk and walk and cry with them. Because when we do, we'll be able to see that, indeed, everyone is beautiful, and we all complement each other so beautifully, and we would all be poorer without each other. Then the saying, "I know you, you're just like me!" will take on a mega-meaning of, "This is 'my family,' and I will stand by them no matter what!"

Stan Dale

Another Way

The train clanked and rattled through the suburbs of Tokyo on a drowsy spring afternoon. Our car was comparatively empty — a few housewives with their kids in tow, some old folks going shopping. I gazed absently at the drab houses and dusty hedgerows.

At one station the doors opened, and suddenly the afternoon quiet was shattered by a man bellowing violent, incomprehensible curses. The man staggered into our car. He wore laborer's clothing and was big, drunk and dirty. Screaming, he swung at a woman holding a baby. The blow sent her spinning into the laps of an elderly couple. It was a miracle that the baby was unharmed.

Terrified, the couple jumped up and scrambled toward the other end of the car. The laborer aimed a kick at the retreating back of the old woman but missed as she scuttled to safety. This so enraged the drunk that he grabbed the metal pole in the center of the car and tried to wrench it out of its stanchion. I could see that one of his hands was cut and bleeding. The train lurched ahead, the passengers frozen with fear. I stood up.

I was young then, some 20 years ago, and in pretty good shape. I'd been putting in a solid eight hours of Aikido training nearly every day for the past three years. I liked to throw and grapple. I thought I was tough. The trouble was, my martial skill was untested in actual combat. As students of Aikido, we were not allowed to fight.

"Aikido," my teacher had said again and again, "is the art of reconciliation. Whoever has the mind to fight has broken his connection with the universe. If you try to dominate people, you're already defeated. We study how to resolve conflict, not how to start it."

I listened to his words. I tried hard. I even went so far as to cross the street to avoid the "chimpira," the pinball punks who lounged around the train stations. My forbearance exalted me. I felt both tough and holy. In my heart, however, I wanted an absolutely legitimate opportunity whereby I might save the innocent by destroying the guilty.

"This is it!" I said to myself as I got to my feet. "People are in danger. If I don't do something fast, somebody will probably get hurt."

Seeing me stand up, the drunk recognized a chance to focus his rage. "Aha!" he roared. "A foreigner! You need a lesson in Japanese manners!"

I held on lightly to the commuter strap overhead and gave him a slow look of disgust and dismissal. I planned to take this turkey apart, but he had to make the first move. I wanted him mad, so I pursed my lips and blew him an insolent kiss.

"All right!" he hollered. "You're gonna get a lesson!" He gathered himself for a rush at me.

A fraction of a second before he could move, someone shouted "Hey!" It was earsplitting. I remember the strangely joyous, lilting quality of it — as though you and a friend had been searching diligently for something, and he had suddenly stumbled upon it. "Hey!"

I wheeled to my left; the drunk spun to his right. We both stared down at a little old Japanese man. He must have been well into his seventies, this tiny gentleman, sitting there immaculate in his kimono. He took no notice of me, but beamed delightedly at the laborer, as though he had a most important, most welcome secret to share.

"C'mere," the old man said in an easy vernacular, beckoning to the drunk. "C'mere and talk with me." He waved his hands lightly.

The big man followed, as if on a string. He planted his feet belligerently in front of the old gentleman and roared above the clacking wheels, "Why the hell should I talk to you?" The drunk now had his back to me. If his elbow moved so much as a millimeter, I'd drop him in his socks.

The old man continued to beam at the laborer. "What'cha been drinkin'?" he asked, his eyes sparkling with interest. "I been drinkin' sake," the laborer bellowed back, "and it's none of your business!" Flecks of spittle spattered the old man.

"Oh, that's wonderful," the old man said, "absolutely wonderful! You see, I love sake, too. Every night, me and my wife (she's 76, you know), we warm up a little bottle of sake and take it out into the garden, and we sit on an old wooden bench. We watch the sun go down, and we look to see how our persimmon tree is doing. My great-grandfather planted that tree, and we worry about whether it will recover from those ice storms we had last winter. Our tree has done better than I expected, though, especially when you consider the poor quality of the soil. It is gratifying to watch when we take our sake and go out to enjoy the evening — even when it rains!" He looked up at the laborer, eyes twinkling.

As he struggled to follow the old man, his face began to soften. His fists slowly unclenched. "Yeah," he said. "I love persimmons, too . . ." His voice trailed off.

"Yes," said the old man, smiling, "and I'm sure you have a wonderful wife."

"No," replied the laborer. "My wife died." Very gently, swaying with the motion of the train, the big man began to sob. "I don't got no wife, I don't got no home, I don't got no job. I'm so ashamed of myself." Tears rolled down his cheeks, a spasm of despair rippled through his body.

As I stood there in my well-scrubbed youthful innocence, my make-this-world-safe-for-democracy righteousness, I felt dirtier than he was.

Then the train arrived at my stop. As the doors opened, I heard the old man cluck sympathetically. "My, my," he said, "that is a difficult predicament indeed. Sit down here and tell me about it."

I turned my head for one last look. The laborer was sprawled on the seat with his head in the old man's lap. The old man was softly stroking the filthy, matted hair.

As the train pulled away, I sat down on a bench in the station. What I had wanted to do with muscle had been accomplished with kind words. I had just seen Aikido in action, and the essence of it was love. I would have to practice the art with an entirely different spirit. It would be a long time before I could speak about the resolution of conflict.

Terry Dobson

The Gentlest Need

At least once a day our old black cat comes to one of us in a way that we've all come to see as a special request. It does not mean he wants to be fed or to be let out or anything of that sort. His need is for something very different.

If you have a lap handy, he'll jump into it; if you don't, he's likely to stand there looking wistful until you make him one. Once in it, he begins to vibrate almost before you stroke his back, scratch his chin and tell him over and over what a good kitty he is. Then his motor really revs up; he squirms to get comfortable; he "makes big hands." Every once in a while one of his purrs gets out of control and turns into a snort. He looks at you with wide open eyes of adoration, and he gives you the cat's long slow blink of ultimate trust.

After a while, little by little, he quiets down. If he senses that it's all right, he may stay in your lap for a cozy nap. But he is just as likely to hop down and stroll away about his business. Either way, he's all right.

Our daughter puts it simply: "Blackie needs to be purred."

In our household he isn't the only one who has that need: I share it and so does my wife. We know the need isn't exclusive to any one age group. Still, because I am a schoolman as well as a parent, I associate it especially with youngsters, with their quick, impulsive need for a hug, a warm lap, a hand held out, a coverlet tucked in, not because anything's wrong, not because anything needs doing, just because that's the way they are.

There are a lot of things I'd like to do for all children. If I could do just one, it would be this: to guarantee every child, everywhere, at least one good purring every day.

Kids, like cats, need time to purr.

Fred T. Wilhelms

Bopsy

The 26-year-old mother stared down at her son who was dying of terminal leukemia. Although her heart was filled with sadness, she also had a strong feeling of determination. Like any parent she wanted her son to grow up and fulfill all his dreams. Now that was no longer possible. The leukemia would see to that. But she still wanted her son's dreams to come true.

She took her son's hand and asked, "Bopsy, did you ever think about what you wanted to be when you grew up? Did you ever dream and wish about what you would do with your life?"

"Mommy, I always wanted to be a fireman when I grew up."

Mom smiled back and said, "Let's see if we can make your wish come true." Later that day she went to her local fire department in Phoenix, Arizona, where she met Fireman Bob, who had a heart as big as Phoenix. She explained her son's final wish and asked if it might be possible to give her six-year-old son a ride around the block on a fire engine.

Fireman Bob said, "Look, we can do better than that. If you'll have your son ready at seven o'clock Wednesday morning, we'll make him an honorary fireman for the whole day. He can come down to the fire station, eat with us, go out on all the fire calls, the whole nine yards! And, if you'll give us his sizes, we'll get a real fire uniform made for him, with a real fire hat — not a toy one — with the emblem of the Phoenix Fire Department on it, a yellow slicker like we wear and rubber boots. They're all manufactured right here in Phoenix, so we can get them fast."

Three days later Fireman Bob picked up Bopsy, dressed him in his fire uniform and escorted him from his hospital bed to the waiting hook and ladder truck. Bopsy got to sit up on the back of the truck and help steer it back to the fire station. He was in heaven.

There were three fire calls in Phoenix that day and Bopsy got to go out on all three calls. He rode in the different fire engines, the paramedics' van and even the fire chief's car. He was also videotaped for the local news program.

Having his dream come true, with all the love and attention that was lavished upon him, so deeply touched Bopsy that he lived three months longer than any doctor thought possible.

One night all of his vital signs began to drop dramatically and the head nurse, who believed in the Hospice concept that no one should die alone, began to call the family members to the hospital. Then she remembered the day Bopsy had spent as a fireman, so she called the fire chief and asked if it would be possible to send a fireman in uniform to the hospital to be with Bopsy as he made his transition. The chief replied, "We can do better than that. We'll be there in five minutes. Will you please do me a favor? When you hear the sirens screaming and see the lights flashing, will you announce over the PA system that there is not a fire? It's just the fire department coming to see one of its finest members one more time. And will you open the window to his room? Thanks."

About five minutes later a hook and ladder truck arrived at the hospital, extended its ladder up to Bopsy's third floor open window and 14 firemen and two firewomen climbed up the ladder into Bopsy's room. With his mother's permission, they hugged him and held him and told him how much they loved him.

With his dying breath, Bopsy looked up at the fire chief and said, "Chief, am I really a fireman now?"

"Bopsy, you are," the chief said.

With those words, Bopsy smiled and closed his eyes for the last time.

Jack Canfield and Mark V. Hansen

REASSURANCE
50¢
Tom Wilson

Puppies For Sale

A store owner was tacking a sign above his door that read "Puppies For Sale." Signs like that have a way of attracting small children, and sure enough, a little boy appeared under the store owner's sign. "How much are you going to sell the puppies for?" he asked.

The store owner replied, "Anywhere from $30 to $50."

The little boy reached in his pocket and pulled out some change. "I have $2.37," he said. "Can I please look at them?"

The store owner smiled and whistled and out of the kennel came Lady, who ran down the aisle of his store followed by five teeny, tiny balls of fur. One puppy was lagging considerably behind. Immediately the little boy singled out the lagging, limping puppy and said, "What's wrong with that little dog?"

The store owner explained that the veterinarian had examined the little puppy and had discovered it didn't have a hip socket. It would always limp. It would always be lame. The little boy became excited. "That is the little puppy that I want to buy."

The store owner said, "No, you don't want to buy that little dog. If you really want him, I'll just give him to you."

The little boy got quite upset. He looked straight into the store owner's eyes, pointing his finger, and said, "I don't want you to give him to me. That little dog is worth every bit as much as all the other dogs and I'll pay full price. In fact, I'll give you $2.37 now, and 50 cents a month until I have him paid for."

The store owner countered, "You really don't want to buy this little dog. He is never going to be able to run and jump and play with you like the other puppies."

To this, the little boy reached down and rolled up his pant leg to reveal a badly twisted, crippled left leg supported by a big metal brace. He looked up at the store owner and softly replied, "Well, I don't run so well myself, and the little puppy will need someone who understands!"

Dan Clark
Weathering the Storm

2

LEARNING TO LOVE YOURSELF

Oliver Wendell Holmes once attended a meeting in which he was the shortest man present.

"Dr. Holmes," quipped a friend, "I should think you'd feel rather small among us big fellows."

"I do," retorted Holmes, "I feel like a dime among a lot of pennies."

The Golden Buddha

And now here is my secret, a very simple secret; it is only with the heart that one can see rightly; what is essential is invisible to the eye.

Antoine de Saint-Exupery

In the fall of 1988 my wife Georgia and I were invited to give a presentation on self-esteem and peak performance at a conference in Hong Kong. Since we had never been to the Far East before, we decided to extend our trip and visit Thailand.

When we arrived in Bangkok, we decided to take a tour of the city's most famous Buddhist temples. Along with our interpreter and driver, Georgia and I visited numerous Buddhist temples that day, but after a while they all began to blur in our memories.

However, there was one temple that left an indelible impression in our hearts and minds. It is called the Temple of the Golden Buddha. The temple itself is very small, probably no larger than thirty feet by thirty feet. But as we entered, we were stunned by the presence of a ten-and-a-half-foot tall, solid-gold Buddha. It weighs over two-and-a-half tons and is valued at approximately one hundred and ninety-six million dollars! It was quite an awesome sight — the kindly gentle, yet imposing solid-gold Buddha smiling down at us.

As we immersed ourselves in the normal sightseeing tasks (taking pictures while oohing and ahhing over the statue), I walked over to a glass case that contained a large piece of clay about eight inches thick and twelve inches wide. Next to the glass case was a typewritten page describing the history of this magnificent piece of art.

Back in 1957 a group of monks from a monastery had to relocate a clay Buddha from their temple to a new location. The monastery was to be relocated to make room for the development of a highway through Bangkok. When the crane began to lift the giant idol, the weight of it was so tremendous that it began to crack. What's more, rain began to fall. The head monk, who was concerned about damage to the sacred Buddha, decided to lower the statue back to the ground and cover it with a large canvas tarp to protect it from the rain.

Later that evening the head monk went to check on the Buddha. He shined his flashlight under the tarp to see if the Buddha was staying dry. As the light reached the crack, he noticed a little gleam shining back and thought it strange. As he took a closer look at this gleam of light, he wondered if there might be something underneath the clay. He went to fetch a chisel and hammer from the monastery and began to chip away at the clay. As he knocked off shards of clay, the little gleam grew brighter and bigger. Many hours of labor went by before the monk stood face to face with the extraordinary solid-gold Buddha.

Historians believe that several hundred years before the head monk's discovery, the Burmese army was about to invade Thailand (then called Siam). The Siamese monks, realizing that their country would soon be attacked, covered their precious golden Buddha with an outer covering of clay in order to keep their treasure from being looted by the Burmese. Unfortunately, it appears that the Burmese slaughtered all the Siamese monks, and the well-kept secret of the golden Buddha remained intact until that fateful day in 1957.

As we flew home on Cathay Pacific Airlines I began to think to myself, "We are all like the clay Buddha covered with a shell of hardness created out of fear, and yet underneath each of us is a 'golden Buddha,' a 'golden Christ' or a 'golden essence,' which is our real self. Somewhere along the way, between the ages of two and nine, we begin to cover up our 'golden essence,' our natural self. Much like the monk with the hammer and the chisel, our task now is to discover our true essence once again."

Jack Canfield

Start With Yourself

The following words were written on the tomb of an Anglican Bishop in the Crypts of Westminister Abbey:

> When I was young and free and my imagination had no limits, I dreamed of changing the world. As I grew older and wiser, I discovered the world would not change, so I shortened my sights somewhat and decided to change only my country.
>
> But it, too, seemed immovable.
>
> As I grew into my twilight years, in one last desperate attempt, I settled for changing only my family, those closest to me, but alas, they would have none of it.
>
> And now as I lie on my deathbed, I suddenly realize: *If I had only changed my self first*, then by example I would have changed my family.
>
> From their inspiration and encouragement, I would then have been able to better my country and, who knows, I may have even changed the world.

Anonymous

Nothing But The Truth!

David Casstevens of the *Dallas Morning News* tells a story about Frank Szymanski, a Notre Dame center in the 1940s, who had been called as a witness in a civil suit at South Bend.

"Are you on the Notre Dame football team this year?" the judge asked.

"Yes, Your Honor."

"What position?"

"Center, Your Honor."

"How good a center?"

Szymanski squirmed in his seat, but said firmly: "Sir, I'm the best center Notre Dame has ever had."

Coach Frank Leahy, who was in the courtroom, was surprised. Szymanski always had been modest and unassuming. So when the proceedings were over, he took Szymanski aside and asked why he had made such a statement. Szymanski blushed.

"I hated to do it, Coach," he said. "But, after all, I *was* under oath."

Covering All The Bases

A little boy was overheard talking to himself as he strode through his backyard, baseball cap in place and toting ball and bat. "I'm the greatest baseball player in the world," he said proudly. Then he tossed the ball in the air, swung and missed. Undaunted, he picked up the ball, threw it into the air and said to himself, "I'm the greatest player ever!" He swung at the ball again, and again he missed. He paused a moment to examine bat and ball carefully. Then once again he threw the ball into the air and said, "I'm the greatest baseball player who ever lived." He swung the bat hard and again missed the ball.

"Wow!" he exclaimed. "What a pitcher!"

Source Unknown

A small child was drawing a picture and his teacher said,
"That's an interesting picture. Tell me about it."
"It's a picture of God."
"But nobody knows what God looks like."
"They will when I get done."

My Declaration Of Self-Esteem

What I am is good enough if I would only be it openly.

Carl Rogers

The following was written in answer to a 15-year-old girl's question, "How can I prepare myelf for a fulfilling life?"

I am me.

In all the world, there is no one else exactly like me. There are people who have some parts like me but no one adds up exactly like me. Therefore, everything that comes out of me is authentically mine because I alone choose it.

I own everything about me — my body, including everything it does; my mind, including all my thoughts and ideas; my eyes, including the images of all they behold; my feelings, whatever they might be — anger, joy, frustration, love, disappointment, excitement; my mouth and all the words that come out of it — polite, sweet or rough, correct or incorrect; my voice, loud or soft; and all my actions, whether they be to others or myself.

I own my own fantasies, my dreams, my hopes, my fears.

I own all my triumphs and successes, all my failures and mistakes.

Because I own all of me, I can become intimately acquainted with me. By so doing, I can love me and be friendly with me in all my parts. I can then make it possible for all of me to work in my best interests.

I know there are aspects about myself that puzzle me, and other aspects that I do not know. But as long as I am friendly and loving to myself, I can courageously and hopefully look for the solutions to the puzzles and for ways to find out more about me.

However I look and sound, whatever I say and do, and whatever I think and feel at a given moment in time is me. This is authentic and represents where I am at that moment in time.

When I review later how I looked and sounded, what I said and did, and how I thought and felt, some parts may turn out to be unfitting. I can discard that which is unfitting and keep that which proved fitting, and invent something new for that which I discarded.

I can see, hear, feel, think, say and do. I have the tools to survive, to be close to others, to be productive, to make sense and order out of the world of people and things outside of me.

I own me and therefore I can engineer me.

I am me and I am okay.

Virginia Satir

The Bag Lady

She used to sleep in the Fifth Street Post Office. I could smell her before I rounded the entrance to where she slept, standing up, by the public phones. I smelled the urine that seeped through the layers of her dirty clothing and the decay from her nearly toothless mouth. If she was not asleep, she mumbled incoherently.

Now they close the post office at six to keep the homeless out, so she curls up on the sidewalk, talking to herself, her mouth flapping open as though unhinged, her smells diminished by the soft breeze.

One Thanksgiving we had so much food left over, I packed it up, excused myself from the others and drove over to Fifth Street.

It was a frigid night. Leaves were swirling around the streets and hardly anyone was out, all but a few of the luckless in some warm home or shelter. But I knew I would find her.

She was dressed as she always was, even in summer: The warm woolly layers concealing her old, bent body. Her bony hands clutched the precious shopping cart. She was squatting against a wire fence in front of the playground next to the post office. "Why didn't she choose some place more protected from the wind?" I thought, and assumed she was so crazy she did not have the sense to huddle in a doorway.

I pulled my shiny car to the curb, rolled down the window and said, "Mother . . . would you . . ." and was shocked at the word "Mother." But she was . . . is . . . in some way I cannot grasp.

I said, again, "Mother, I've brought you some food. Would you like some turkey and stuffing and apple pie?"

At this the old woman looked at me and said quite clearly and distinctly, her two loose lower teeth wobbling as she spoke, "Oh, thank you very much, but I'm quite full now. Why don't you take it to someone who really needs it?" Her words were clear, her manners gracious. Then I was dismissed: Her head sank into her rags again.

Bobbie Probstein

Response/Ability

the game we play
is let's pretend
and pretend
we're not
pretending

we choose to
forget
who we are
and then forget
that we've
forgotten

who are we really?

the center
that watches
and runs the show
that can choose
which way
it will go

the I AM
consciousness
that powerful
loving perfect
reflection
of the cosmos

but in our attempt
to cope with
early situations
we chose or were
hypnotized into
a passive position

to avoid
punishment
or the loss of love
we chose to deny
our
response/ability
pretending that

things just
happened
or that we were
being controlled
taken over

we put ourselves
down
and have become
used to this
masochistic
posture
this weakness
this indecisiveness

but we are
in reality
free
a center
of cosmic energy

your will
is your power

don't pretend
you don't have it

or you won't

Bernard Gunther

The Rules For Being Human

1. **You will receive a body.**
   You may like it or hate it, but it will be yours for the entire period of this time around.
2. **You will learn lessons.**
   You are enrolled in a full-time informal school called Life. Each day in this school you will have the opportunity to learn lessons. You may like the lessons or think them irrelevant and stupid.
3. **There are no mistakes, only lessons.**
   Growth is a process of trial and error: Experimentation. The "failed" experiments are as much a part of the process as the experiment that ultimately "works."
4. **A lesson is repeated until learned.**
   A lesson will be presented to you in various forms until you have learned it. When you have learned it, you can then go on to the next lesson.
5. **Learning lessons does not end.**
   There is no part of life that does not contain its lessons. If you are alive, there are lessons to be learned.
6. **"There" is no better than "here."**
   When your "there" has become a "here," you

will simply obtain another "there" that will again look better than "here."

7. **Others are merely mirrors of you.**
   You cannot love or hate something about another person unless it reflects something you love or hate about yourself.
8. **What you make of your life is up to you.**
   You have all the tools and resources you need. What you do with them is up to you. The choice is yours.
9. **Your answers lie inside you.**
   The answers to Life's questions lie inside you. All you need to do is look, listen and trust.
10. **You will forget all this.**

Chérie Carter-Scott

3

ON PARENTING

Perhaps the greatest social service that can be rendered by anybody to the country and to mankind is to bring up a family.

George Bernard Shaw

Children Learn What They Live

If children live with criticism,
  they learn to condemn.

If children live with hostility,
  they learn to fight.

If children live with fear,
  they learn to be apprehensive.

If children live with pity,
  they learn to feel sorry for themselves.

If children live with ridicule,
  they learn to be shy.

If children live with jealousy,
  they learn what envy is.

If children live with shame,
  they learn to feel guilty.

If children live with tolerance,
  they learn to be patient.

If children live with encouragement,
  they learn to be confident.

If children live with praise,
  they learn to appreciate.

If children live with approval,
  they learn to like themselves.

If children live with acceptance,
  they learn to find love in the world.

If children live with recognition,
  they learn to have a goal.

If children live with sharing,
  they learn to be generous.

If children live with honesty and fairness,
  they learn what truth and justice are.

If children live with security,
  they learn to have faith in themselves
  and in those around them.

If children live with friendliness,
  they learn that the world is a nice
  place in which to live.

If children live with serenity,
  they learn to have peace of mind.

With what are your children living?

Dorothy L. Nolte

Why I Chose My Father To Be My Dad

I grew up on a beautiful sprawling farm in Iowa, raised by parents who are often described as the "salt of the earth and the backbone of the community." They were all the things we know good parents to be: loving, committed to the task of raising their children with high expectations and a positive sense of self-regard. They expected us to do morning and evening chores, get to school on time, get decent grades and be good people.

There are six children. *Six* children! It was never my idea that there should be so many of us, but then no one consulted me. To make matters worse, fate dropped me off in the middle of the American heartland in a most harsh and cold climate. Like all children, I thought that there had been a great universal mistake and I had been placed in the wrong family — most definitely in the wrong state. I disliked coping with the elements. The winters in Iowa are so freezing cold that you have to make rounds in the middle of the night to see that livestock aren't stranded in a place where they would freeze to death. Newborn animals had to be taken in the barn and sometimes warmed up in order to be kept alive. Winters are *that* cold in Iowa!

My dad, an incredibly handsome, strong, charismatic and energetic man was always in motion. My brothers and sisters and I were in awe of him. We honored him and held him in the highest esteem. Now I understand why. There were no inconsistencies in his life. He was an honorable man, highly principled. Farming, his chosen work, was his passion; he was the best. He was at home raising and caring for animals. He felt at one with the earth and took great pride in planting and harvesting the crops. He refused to hunt out of season, even though deer, pheasants, quail and other game roamed our farmlands in abundance. He refused to use soil additives or feed the animals anything other than natural grains. He taught us why he did this and why we must embrace the same ideals. Today I can see how conscientious he was because this was in the mid '50s before there was an attempt at universal commitment to earth-wide environmental preservation.

Dad was also a very impatient man, but not in the middle of the night when he was checking his animals during these late night rounds. The relationship we developed from these times together was simply unforgettable. It made a compelling difference in my life. I learned so much *about* him. I often hear men and women say they spent so little time with their fathers. Indeed the heart of today's men's groups is about groping for a father they never really knew. I knew mine.

Back then I felt as if I was secretly his favorite child, although it's quite possible that each of us six children felt that way. Now that was both good news and bad. The bad news was that I was the one selected by Dad to go with him for these midnight and early morning barnyard checks, and I absolutely detested getting up and leaving a warm bed to go out into the frosty air. But my dad was at his best and most lovable during those times. He was most understanding, patient, gentle and was a good listener. His voice was gentle and his smile made me understand my mother's passion for him.

It was during these times when he was a model teacher — always focusing on the whys, the reasons for doing. He talked endlessly for the hour or hour-and-a-half that it took to make the rounds. He talked about his war experiences, the whys of the war he served in and about the region, its people, the effects of war and its aftermath. Again and again he told his story. In school I found history all the more exciting and familiar.

He talked about what he gained from his travels and why seeing the world was so important. He instilled a need and love of traveling. I had worked in or visited some 30 countries by the time I was 30 years old.

He talked about the need and love of learning and why a formal education is important, and he talked about the difference between intelligence and wisdom. He wanted so much for me to go beyond my high school degree. "You can do it," he'd say over and over. "You're a Burres. You are bright, you have a good mind and, remember, you're a Burres." There was no way I was going to let him down. I had more than enough confidence to tackle any course of study. Eventually I completed a Ph.D. and later earned a second doctorate. Though the first doctorate was for Dad and the second for me, there was definitely a sense of curiosity and quest that made both easy to attain.

He talked about standards and values, developing character and what it meant in the course of one's life. I write and teach on a similar theme. He talked about how to make and evaluate decisions, when to cut your losses and walk away and when to stick it out, even in the face of adversity. He talked about the concept of *being and becoming* and not just *having and getting*. I still use that phrase. "Never sell out on your heart," he said. He talked about gut instincts and how to decipher between those and emotional sells, and how to avoid being fooled by others. He said, "Always listen to your instincts and know that all the answers you'll ever need are within you. Take quiet time alone. Be still enough to find the answers within and then listen to them. Find something you love to do, then live a life that shows it. Your goals should stem from your values, and then your work will radiate your heart's desire. This will divert you from all silly distractions that will only serve to waste your time — your very life is about time — how much you can grow in whatever years you are given. Care about people," he said, "and always respect mother earth. Wherever you shall live, be sure you have full view of the trees, sky and land."

My father. When I reflect on how he loved and valued his children, I'm genuinely sorry for the youth who will never know their fathers in this way or will never feel the power of character, ethics, drive and sensitivity all in one person — as I do in mine. My dad modeled what he talked. And I always knew he was serious about me. I knew he felt me worthy, and he wanted me to see that worth.

Dad's message made sense to me because I never saw any conflict in the way he lived his life. He had thought about his life and he lived it daily. He bought and paid for several farms over time (he's as active today as he was then). He married and has loved the same woman for a lifetime. My mother and he, now married for nearly 50 years, are still inseparable sweethearts. They are the greatest lovers I've known. And he loved his family so much. I thought he was overly possessive and protective of his children, but now that I'm a parent I can understand those needs and see them for what they are. Though he thought he could save us from the measles and almost did, he vehemently refused to lose us to destructive vices. I also see how determined he was that we be caring and responsible adults.

To this day five of his children live within a few miles of him, and they have chosen a version of his lifestyle. They are devoted spouses and parents, and agriculture is their chosen work. They are without a doubt, the backbone of their community. There is a twist to all this, and I suspect it's because of his taking me on those midnight rounds. I took a different direction than did the other five children. I began a career as an educator, counselor and university professor, eventually writing several books for parents and children to share what I had learned about the importance of developing self-esteem in the childhood years. My messages to my daughter, while altered a bit, are the values that I learned from my father, tempered with my life experiences, of course. They continue to be passed on.

I should tell you a bit about my daughter. She's a tomboy, a beautiful 5 foot 9 athlete who letters in three sports each year, frets over the difference between an A- and a B, and was just named a finalist in the Miss Teen California contest. But it's not her outward gifts and accomplishments that remind me of my parents. People always tell me that my daughter possesses a great kindness, a spirituality, a special fire deep inside that radiates outward. The essence of my parents is personified in their granddaughter.

The rewards of esteeming their children and being dedicated parents have had a most nourishing effect on the lives of my parents as well. As of this writing, my father is at the Mayo Clinic in Rochester, Minnesota, for a battery of tests, scheduled to take from six to eight days. It is December. Because of the harsh winter, he took a hotel room near the clinic (as an outpatient). Because of obligations at home, my mother was only able to stay with him for the first few days. So on Christmas Eve, they were apart.

That night I first called my dad in Rochester to say Merry Christmas. He sounded down and despondent. Then, I called my mother in Iowa. She was sad and morose. "This is the first time your father and I have ever spent the holidays apart," she lamented. "It's just not Christmas without him."

I had 14 dinner guests arriving, all ready for a festive evening. I returned to cooking, but not being able to get my parents' dilemma fully off my mind, I called my older sister. She called my brothers. We conferenced by phone. It was settled. Determined that our parents should not be without each other on Christmas Eve, my younger brother would drive the two hours to Rochester to pick up my father and bring him home without telling my mother. I called my father to tell him of the plans. "Oh, no," he said, "it's far too dangerous to come out on a night like this." My brother arrived in Rochester and knocked at my father's hotel door. He called me from Dad's room to tell me he wouldn't go. "You have to tell him, Bobbie. You're the only one he'll listen to."

"Go, Dad," I said gently.

He did. Tim and my dad started for Iowa. We kids kept track of their progress, the journey and the weather by talking with them on my brother's car phone. By now, all my guests had arrived and all were a part of this ordeal. Whenever the phone rang, we put it on the speaker phone so we could hear the latest! It was just past 9:00 when the phone rang and it was Dad on the car phone, "Bobbie, how can I possibly go home without a gift for your mom? It would be the first time in nearly 50 years I didn't get her perfume for Christmas!" By now my entire dinner party was engineering this plan. We called my sister to get the names of nearby open shopping centers so they could stop for the only gift my dad would consider giving Mom — the same brand of perfume he has given her every year at Christmas.

At 9:52 that evening, my brother and my dad left a little shopping mall in Minnesota for the trip home. At 11:50 they drove into the farmstead. My father, acting like a giggling school boy, stepped around the corner of the house and stood out of sight.

"Mom, I visited Dad today and he said to bring you his laundry," my brother said as he handed my mom the suitcases.

"Oh," she said softly and sadly, "I miss him so much, I might as well do these now."

Said my father coming out from his hiding, "You won't have time to do them tonight."

After my brother called me to relay this touching scene between our parents — these two friends and lovers — I phoned my mother. "Merry Christmas, Mother!"

"Oh, you kids . . .," she said in a crackling voice choking back tears. She was unable to continue. My guests cheered.

Though I was 2,000 miles away from them, it was one of the most special Christmases I've shared with my parents. And, of course, to date my parents have not been apart on Christmas Eve. That's the strength of children who love and honor their parents and, of course, the committed and marvelous marriage my parents share.

"Good parents," Jonas Salk once told me, "give their children roots and wings. Roots to know where home is, wings to fly away and exercise what's been taught them." If gaining the skills to lead one's life purposefully and having a safe nest and being welcomed back to it is the legacy of parents, then I believe I chose my parents well. It was this past Christmas that I most fully understood why it was necessary that these two people be my parents. Though wings have taken me around the globe, eventually to nest in lovely California, the roots my parents gave me will be an indelible foundation forever.

Bettie B. Youngs

The Animal School

Once upon a time, the animals decided they must do something heroic to meet the problems of "a new world." So they organized a school.

They adopted an activity curriculum consisting of running, climbing, swimming and flying. To make it easier to administer the curriculum, all the animals took all the subjects.

The duck was excellent in swimming, in fact better than his instructor, but he made only passing grades in flying and was very poor in running. Since he was slow in running, he had to stay after school and also drop swimming in order to practice running. This was kept up until his webbed feet were badly worn and he was only average in swimming. But average was acceptable in school, so nobody worried about that except the duck.

The rabbit started at the top of the class in running, but had a nervous breakdown because of so much make-up work in swimming.

The squirrel was excellent in climbing until he developed frustration in the flying class where his teacher made him start from the ground up instead of from the treetop down. He also developed a "charlie horse" from overexertion and then got a C in climbing and a D in running.

The eagle was a problem child and was disciplined severely. In the climbing class he beat all the others to the top of the tree, but insisted on using his own way to get there.

At the end of the year, an abnormal eel that could swim exceedingly well, and also run, climb and fly a little, had the highest average and was valedictorian.

The prairie dogs stayed out of school and fought the tax levy because the administration would not add digging and burrowing to the curriculum. They apprenticed their children to a badger and later joined the groundhogs and gophers to start a successful private school.

Does this fable have a moral?

George H. Reavis

Touched

She is my daughter and is immersed in the turbulence of her 16th year. Following a recent bout with illness, she learned her best friend would soon be moving away. School was not going as well as she had hoped, nor as well as her mother and I had hoped. She exuded sadness through a muffle of blankets as she huddled in bed, searching for comfort. I wanted to reach out to her and wrench away all the miseries that had taken root in her young spirit. Yet, even aware of how much I cared for her and wanted to remove her unhappiness, I knew the importance of proceeding with caution.

As a family therapist I've been well-educated about inappropriate expressions of intimacy between fathers and daughters, primarily by clients whose lives have been torn apart by sexual abuse. I'm also aware of how easily care and closeness can be sexualized, especially by men who find the emotional field foreign territory and who mistake any expression of affection for sexual invitation. How much easier it was to hold and comfort her when she was two or three or even seven. But now her body, our society and my manhood all seemed to conspire against my comforting my daughter. How could I console her while still respecting the necessary boundaries between a father and a teenage daughter? I settled for offering her a back rub. She consented.

I gently massaged her bony back and knotted shoulders as I apologized for my recent absence. I explained that I had just returned from the international back-rubbing finals, where I had placed fourth. I assured her that it's hard to beat the back rub of a concerned father, especially if he's a world class back rubbing concerned father. I told her all about the contest and the other contestants as my hands and fingers sought to loosen tightened muscles and unlock the tensions in her young life.

I told her about the shrunken antique Asian man who had placed third in the contest. After studying acupuncture and acupressure his entire life, he could focus all his energy into his fingers, elevating back rubbing to an art. "He poked and prodded with prestidigitatious precision," I explained, showing my daughter a sample of what I'd learned from the old man. She groaned, though I wasn't sure whether in response to my alliteration or my touch. Then I told her about the woman who had placed second. She was from Turkey and since her childhood had practiced the art of belly dancing, so she could make muscles move and ripple in fluid motion. With her back rub, her fingers awakened in tired muscles and weary bodies an urge to vibrate and quiver and dance. "She let her fingers do the walking and the muscles tagged along," I said, demonstrating.

"That's weird," emanated faintly from a face muffled by a pillow. Was it my one-liner or my touch?

Then I just rubbed my daughter's back and we settled into silence. After a time she asked, "So who got first place?"

"You'd never believe it!" I said. "It was baby!" And I explained how the soft, trusting touches of an infant exploring a world of skin and smells and tastes was like no other touch in the world. Softer than soft. Unpredictable, gentle, searching. Tiny hands saying more than words could ever express. About belonging. About trust. About innocent love. And then I gently and softly touched her as I had learned from the infant. I recalled vividly her own infancy — holding her, rocking her, watching her grope and grow into her world. I realized that she, in fact, was the infant who had taught me about the touch of the infant.

After another period of gentle back rubbing and silence, I said I was glad to have learned so much from the world's expert back rubbers. I explained how I had become an even better back rubber for a 16-year-old daughter painfully stretching herself into adult shape. I offered a silent prayer of thanks that such life had been placed in my hands and that I was blessed with the miracle of touching even a part of it.

Victor Nelson

I Love You, Son

Thoughts while driving my son to school: Morning, Kid. You look pretty sharp in your Cub Scout gear, not as fat as your old man when he was a Cub. I don't think my hair was ever as long until I went away to college, but I think I'd recognize you any way by what you are: a little shaggy around the ears, scuffed around the toes, wrinkled in the knees . . . We get used to one another . . .

Now that you're eight I notice I don't see a whole lot of you anymore. On Columbus Day you left at nine in the morning. I saw you for 42 seconds at lunch and you reappeared for supper at five. I miss you, but I know you've got serious business to take care of. Certainly as serious as, if not more important than, the things the other commuters on the road are doing.

You've got to grow up and out and that's more important than clipping coupons, arranging stock options or selling people short. You've got to learn what you are able to do and what you aren't — and you've got to learn how to deal with that. You've got to learn about people and how they behave when they don't feel good about themselves — like the bullies who hang out at the bike rack and hassle the smaller kids. Yeah, you'll even have to learn how to pretend that name-calling doesn't hurt. It'll always hurt, but you'll have to put up a front or they'll call you worse names next time. I only hope you remember how it feels — in case you ever decide to rank a kid who's smaller than you.

When was the last time I told you I was proud of you? I guess if I can't remember, I've got work to do. I remember the last time I yelled at you — told you we'd be late if you didn't hurry — but, on balance, as Nixon used to say, I haven't given you as many pats as yells. For the record, in case you read this, I am proud of you. I especially like your independence, the way you take care of yourself even when it frightens me just a little bit. You've never been much of a whiner and that makes you a superior kid in my book.

Why is it that fathers are so slow to realize that eight-year-olds need as many hugs as four-year-olds? If I don't watch out, pretty soon I'll be punching you on the arm and saying, "Whaddaya say, kid?!" instead of hugging you and telling you I love you. Life is too short to hide affection. Why is it that eight-year-olds are so slow to realize that 36-year-olds need as many hugs as four-year-olds?

Did I forget to tell you that I'm proud you went back to a box lunch after one week's worth of that indigestible hot lunch? I'm glad you value your body.

I wish the drive weren't so short . . . I want to talk about last night . . . when your younger brother was asleep and we let you stay up and watch the Yankees game. Those times are so special. There's no way you can plan them. Every time we try to plan something together, it's not as good or rich or warm. For a few all-too short minutes it was as if you'd already grown up and we sat and talked without any words about "How are you doing in school, son?" I'd already checked your math homework the only way

I could — with a calculator. You're better with numbers than I'll ever be. So, we talked about the game and you knew more about the players than I did and I learned from you. And we were both happy when the Yankees won.

Well, there's the crossing guard. He'll probably outlive all of us. I wish you didn't have to go to school today. There are so many things I want to say.

Your exit from my car is so quick. I want to savor the moment and you've already spotted a couple of your friends.

I just wanted to say "I love you, son . . ."

Victor B. Miller

What You Are Is As Important As What You Do

Who you are speaks so loudly I can't hear what you're saying.

Ralph Waldo Emerson

It was a sunny Saturday afternoon in Oklahoma City. My friend and proud father Bobby Lewis was taking his two little boys to play miniature golf. He walked up to the fellow at the ticket counter and said, "How much is it to get in?"

The young man replied, "$3.00 for you and $3.00 for any kid who is older than six. We let them in free if they are six or younger. How old are they?"

Bobby replied, "The lawyer's three and the doctor is seven, so I guess I owe you $6.00."

The man at the ticket counter said, "Hey, Mister, did you just win the lottery or something? You could have saved yourself three bucks. You could have told me that the older one was six; I wouldn't have known the difference." Bobby replied, "Yes, that may be true, but the kids would have known the difference."

As Ralph Waldo Emerson said, "Who you are speaks so loudly I can't hear what you're saying." In challenging times when ethics are more important than ever before, make sure you set a good example for everyone you work and live with.

Patricia Fripp

A Mom's Life

Take your plate into the kitchen, please.
Take it downstairs when you go.
Don't leave it there, take it upstairs.
Is that yours?
Don't hit your brother.
I'm talking to you.
Just a minute, please, can't you see I'm talking?
I said, Don't interrupt.
Did you brush your teeth?
What are you doing out of bed?
Go back to bed.
You can't watch in the afternoon.
What do you mean, there's nothing to do?
Go outside.
Read a book.
Turn it down.
Get off the phone.
Tell your friend you'll call her back. Right now!
Hello. No, she's not home.
She'll call you when she gets home.
Take a jacket. Take a sweater.
Take one anyway.
Someone left his shoes in front of the TV.
Get the toys out of the hall. Get the boys out of the bathtub. Get the toys off the stairs.

Do you realize that could kill someone?
Hurry up.
Hurry up. Everyone's waiting.
I'll count to ten and then we're going without you.
Did you go to the bathroom?
If you don't go, you're not going.
I mean it.
Why didn't you go before you left?
Can you hold it?
What's going on back there?
Stop it.
I said, Stop it!
I don't want to hear about it.
Stop it or I'm taking you home right now.
That's it. We're going home.
Give me a kiss.
I need a hug.
Make your bed.
Clean up your room.
Set the table.
I need you to set the table!
Don't tell me it's not your turn.
Please move your chair in to the table.
Sit up.
Just try a little. You don't have to eat the whole thing.
Stop playing and eat.
Would you watch what you're doing?
Move your glass. It's too close to the edge.
Watch it!
More, what?
More, please. That's better.
Just eat one bite of salad.
You don't always get what you want. That's life.
Don't argue with me. I'm not discussing this anymore.
Go to your room.

No, ten minutes are not up.
One more minute.
How many times have I told you, don't do that.
Where did the cookies go?
Eat the old fruit before you eat the new fruit.
I'm not giving you mushrooms. I've taken all the mushrooms out. See?
Is your homework done?
Stop yelling. If you want to ask me something, come here.
STOP YELLING. IF YOU WANT TO ASK ME SOMETHING, COME HERE.
I'll think about it.
Not now.
Ask your father.
We'll see.
Don't sit so close to the television, it's bad for your eyes.
Calm down.
Calm down and start over.
Is that the truth?
Fasten your seat belt.
Did everyone fasten their seat belts?
I'm sorry, that's the rule. I'm sorry, that's the rule. I'm sorry, that's the rule.

Delia Ephron

The Perfect American Family

It is 10:30 on a perfect Saturday morning and we are, for the moment, the perfect American family. My wife has taken our six-year-old to his first piano lesson. Our 14-year-old has not yet roused from his slumber. The four-year-old watches tiny, anthropomorphic beings hurl one another from cliffs in the other room. I sit at the kitchen table reading the newspaper.

Aaron Malachi, the four-year-old, apparently bored by the cartoon carnage and the considerable personal power obtained by holding the television's remote control, enters my space.

"I'm hungry," he says.

"Want some more cereal?"

"No."

"Want some yogurt?"

"No."

"Want some eggs?"

"No. Can I have some ice cream?"

"No."

For all I know, ice cream may be far more nourishing than processed cereal or antibiotic-laden eggs but, according to my cultural values, it is wrong to have ice cream at 10:45 on a Saturday morning.

Silence. About four seconds. "Daddy, we have very much of life left, don't we?"

"Yes, we have lots of life left, Aaron."

"Me and you and Mommy?"

"That's right."

"And Isaac?"

"Yes."

"And Ben?"

"Yes. You and me and Mommy and Isaac and Ben."

"We have very much of life left. Until all the people die."

"What do you mean?"

"Until all the people die and the dinosaurs come back."

Aaron sits down on the table, cross-legged like a Buddha, in the center of my newspaper.

"What do you mean, Aaron, 'until all the people die'?"

"You said everybody dies. When everybody dies, then the dinosaurs will come back. The cavemen lived in caves, dinosaur caves. Then the dinosaurs came back and squished 'em."

I realize that already for Aaron life is a limited economy, a resource with a beginning and an end. He envisions himself and us somewhere along that trajectory, a trajectory that ends in uncertainty and loss.

I am faced with an ethical decision. What should I do now? Should I attempt to give him God, salvation, eternity? Should I toss him some spiel like, "Your body is just a shell and after you die, we will all be together in spirit forever"?

Or should I leave him with his uncertainty and his anxiety because I think it's real? Should I try to make him an anxious existentialist or should I try to make him feel better?

I don't know. I stare at the newspaper. The Celtics are consistently losing on Friday nights. Larry Bird is angry at somebody, but I can't see who, because Aaron's foot is in the way. I don't know but my neurotic, addictive, middle-class sensibility is telling me that this is a very important moment, a moment when Aaron's ways of constructing his world are being formed. Or maybe my neurotic, addictive, middle-class sensibility is just making me think that. If life and death are an illusion, then why should I trifle with how someone else understands them?

On the table Aaron plays with an "army guy," raising his arms and balancing him on his shaky legs. It was Kevin McHale that Larry Bird was angry at. No, not Kevin McHale, it was Jerry Sichting. But Jerry Sichting is no longer with the Celtics. Whatever happened to Jerry Sichting? Everything dies, everything comes to an end. Jerry Sichting is playing for Sacramento or Orlando or he has disappeared.

I should not trifle with how Aaron understands life and death because I want him to have a solid sense of structure, a sense of the permanence of things. It's obvious what a good job the nuns and priests did with me. It was agony or bliss. Heaven and hell were not connected by long distance service. You were on God's team or you were in the soup, and the soup was hot. I don't want Aaron to get burned, but I want him to have a strong frame. The neurotic but unavoidable anxiety can come later.

Is that possible? Is it possible to have a sense that God, spirit, karma, Y*W*H, something — is transcendent, without traumatizing the presentness of a person, without beating it into them? Can we have our cake and eat it too, ontologically speaking? Or is their fragile sensibility, their "there-ness," sundered by such an act?

Sensing a slight increase in agitation on the table, I know that Aaron is becoming bored with his guy. With an attitude of drama benefiting the moment, I clear my throat and begin with a professional tone.

"Aaron, death is something that some people believe . . ."

"Dad," Aaron interrupts, "could we play a video game? It's not a very violent game," he explains, hands gesticulating. "It's not like a killing game. The guys just kind of flop over."

"Yes," I say with some relief, "let's play video games. But first there's something else we have to do."

"What?" Aaron stops and turns from where he has run, already halfway to the arcade.

"First, let's have some ice cream."

Another perfect Saturday for a perfect family. For now.

Michael Murphy

I'd just like to say
Before I go to sleep,
I'm sorry today
I acted like a creep!

Illustration by Adrian Carranza.
Prayer Reprinted by Special Permission of Guideposts *magazine.*

Just Say It!

If you were going to die soon and had only one phone call you could make, who would you call and what would you say? And why are you waiting?

Stephen Levine

One night, after reading one of the hundreds of parenting books I've read, I was feeling a little guilty because the book had described some parenting strategies I hadn't used in a while. The main strategy was to talk with your child and use those three magic words: "I love you." It had stressed over and over that children need to know that unconditionally and unequivocally that you *really* love them.

I went upstairs to my son's bedroom and knocked on the door. As I knocked, all I could hear were his drums. I knew he was there but he wasn't answering. So I opened the door and, sure enough, there he was sitting with his earphones on, listening to a tape and playing his drums. After I leaned over to get his attention, I said to him, "Tim, have you got a second?"

He said "Oh sure, Dad. I'm always good for one." We proceeded to sit down and after about 15 minutes and a lot of small talk and stuttering, I just looked at him and said, "Tim, I really love the way you play drums."

He said, "Oh, thanks, Dad, I appreciate it."

I walked out of the door and said, "See you later!" As I was walking downstairs, it dawned on me that I went up there with a certain message and had not delivered it. I felt it was really important to get back up there and have another chance to say those three magic words.

Again I climbed the stairs, knocked on the door and opened it. "You got a second, Tim?"

"Sure, Dad. I'm always good for a second or two. What do you need?"

"Son, the first time I came up here to share a message with you, something else came out. It really wasn't what I wanted to share with you. Tim, do you remember when you were learning how to drive, it caused me a lot of problems? I wrote three words and slipped them under your pillow in hopes that would take care of it. I'd done my part as a parent and expressed my love to my son." Finally after a little small talk, I looked at Tim and said, "What I want you to know is that we love you."

He looked at me and said, "Oh, thanks, Dad. That's you and Mom?"

I said, "Yeah, that's both of us, we just don't express it enough."

He said, "Thanks, that means a lot. I know you do."

I turned around and walked out the door. As I was walking downstairs, I started thinking, "I can't believe this. I've already been up there twice — I know what the message is and yet something else comes out of my mouth."

I decided I'm going back there now and let Tim know exactly how I feel. He's going to hear it directly from me. I don't care if he is six feet tall! So back I go, knock on the door and he yells "Wait a minute. Don't tell me who it is. Could that be you, Dad?"

I said, "How'd you know that?" and he responded, "I've known you ever since you were a parent, Dad."

Then I said "Son, have you got just one more second?"

"You know I'm good for one, so come on in. I suppose you didn't tell me what you wanted to tell me?"

I said, "How'd you know that?"

"I've known you ever since I was in diapers."

I said, "Well, here it is, Tim, what I've been holding back on. I just want to express to you how special you are to our family. It's not what you do, and it's not what you've done, like all the things you're doing with the junior high kids in town. It's who you are as a person. I love you and I just wanted you to know I love you, and I don't know why I hold back on something so important."

He looked at me and he said, "Hey, Dad, I know you do and it's really special hearing you say it to me. Thanks so much for your thoughts, as well as the intent." As I was walking out the door, he said, "Oh, hey, Dad. Have you got another second?"

I started thinking, "Oh no. What's he going to say to me?" I said, "Oh sure. I'm always good for one."

I don't know where kids get this — I'm sure it couldn't be from their parents, but he said, "Dad, I just want to ask you one question."

I said, "What's that?"

He looked at me and said, "Dad, have you been to a workshop or something like that?"

I'm thinking, "Oh no, like any other 18-year-old, he's got my number," and I said, "No, I was reading a book, and it said how important it is to tell your kids how you really feel about them."

"Hey, thanks for taking the time. Talk to you later, Dad."

I think what Tim taught me, more than anything else that night is that the only way you can understand the real meaning and purpose of love is to be willing to pay the price. You have to go out there and risk sharing it.

Gene Bedley

A Legacy Of Love

As a young man, Al was a skilled artist, a potter. He had a wife and two fine sons. One night, his oldest son developed a severe stomachache. Thinking it was only some common intestinal disorder, neither Al nor his wife took the condition very seriously. But the malady was actually acute appendicitis, and the boy died suddenly that night.

Knowing the death could have been prevented if he had only realized the seriousness of the situation, Al's emotional health deteriorated under the enormous burden of his guilt. To make matters worse his wife left him a short time later, leaving him alone with his six-year-old younger son. The hurt and pain of the two situations were more than Al could handle, and he turned to alcohol to help him cope. In time Al became an alcoholic.

As the alcoholism progressed, Al began to lose everything he possessed — his home, his land, his art objects, everything. Eventually Al died alone in a San Francisco motel room.

When I heard of Al's death, I reacted with the same disdain the world shows for one who ends his life with nothing material to show for it. "What a complete failure!" I thought. "What a totally wasted life!"

As time went by, I began to re-evaluate my earlier harsh judgment. You see, I knew Al's now adult son, Ernie. He is one of the kindest, most caring, most loving men I have ever known. I watched Ernie with his children and saw the free flow of love between them. I knew that kindness and caring had to come from somewhere.

I hadn't heard Ernie talk much about his father. It is so hard to defend an alcoholic. One day I worked up my courage to ask him. "I'm really puzzled by something," I said. "I know your father was basically the only one to raise you. What on earth did he do that you became such a special person?"

Ernie sat quietly and reflected for a few moments. Then he said, "From my earliest memories as a child until I left home at 18, Al came into my room every night, gave me a kiss and said, 'I love you, son.' "

Tears came to my eyes as I realized what a fool I had been to judge Al as a failure. He had not left any material possessions behind. But he had been a kind loving father, and he left behind one of the finest, most giving men I have ever known.

Bobbie Gee
Winning The Image Game

On Parenting

Your children are not your children.
They are the sons and daughters of Life's longing for itself.
They come through you but not from you,
And though they are with you, yet they belong not to you.
You may give them your love but not your thoughts,
For they have their own thoughts.
You may house their bodies but not their souls,
For their souls dwell in the house of tomorrow, which you cannot visit, not even in your dreams.
You may strive to be like them, but seek not to make them like you,
For life goes not backward nor tarries with yesterday.
You are the bows from which your children as living arrows are sent forth.
The archer sees the mark upon the path of the infinite, and He bends you with His might that His arrows might go swift and far.
Let your bending in the archer's hand be for gladness;
For even as He loves the arrow that flies, so He loves also the bow that is stable.

Kahlil Gibran

4

ON LEARNING

Learning is finding out
what you already know.

Doing is demonstrating
that you know it.

Teaching is reminding
others that they know it
just as well as you.

You are all learners,
doers, teachers.

Richard Bach

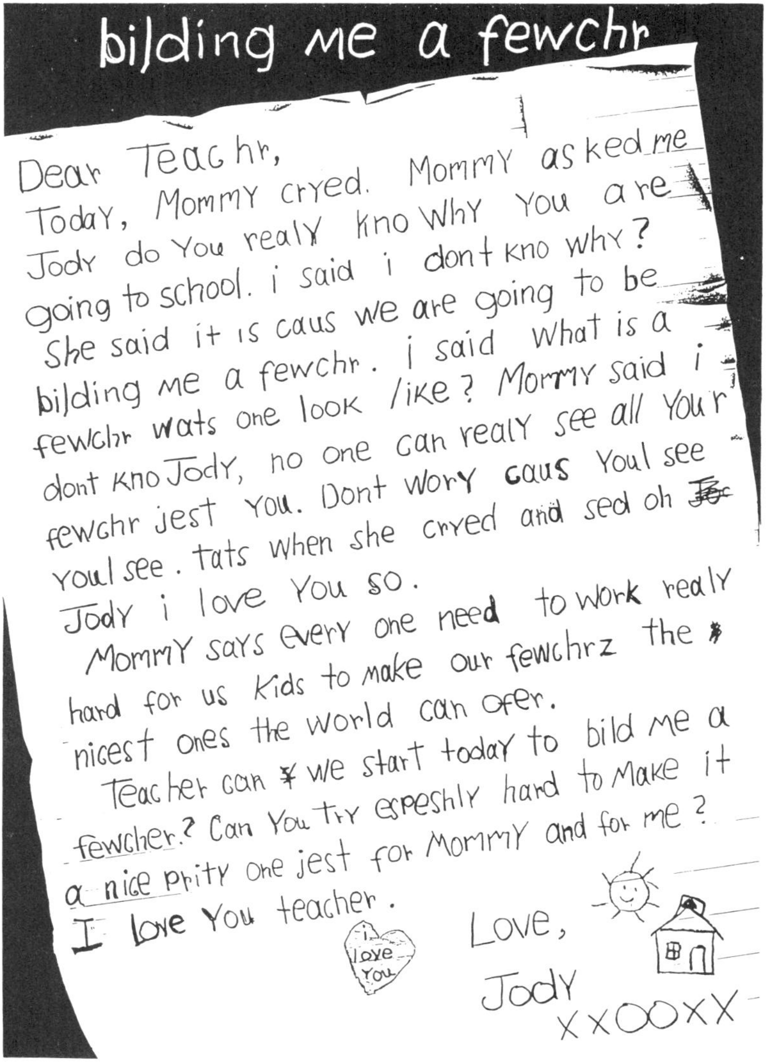

bilding me a fewchr

Dear Teachr,
Today, Mommy cryed. Mommy asked me
Jody do You realy kno Why You are
going to school. i said i dont kno why?
She said it is caus we are going to be
bilding me a fewchr. i said What is a
fewchr wats one look like? Mommy said i
dont kno Jody, no one can realy see all Your
fewchr jest You. Dont wory caus Youl see
Youl see. tats when she cryed and sed oh ~~Jo~~
Jody i love You so.
Mommy says every one need to work realy
hard for us Kids to make our fewchrz the
nicest ones the world can ofer.
Teacher can we start today to bild me a
fewcher? Can You try espeshly hard to Make it
a nice prity one jest for Mommy and for me?
I love You teacher.

Love,
Jody
XXOOXX

Authored by Frank Trujillo

I Like Myself Now

Once you see a child's self-image begin to improve, you will see significant gains in achievement areas, but even more important, you will see a child who is beginning to enjoy life more.

Wayne Dyer

I had a great feeling of relief when I began to understand that a youngster needs more than just subject matter. I know mathematics well, and I teach it well. I used to think that was all I needed to do. Now I teach children, not math. I accept the fact that I can only succeed partially with some of them. When I don't have to know all the answers, I seem to have more answers than when I tried to be the expert. The youngster who really made me understand this was Eddie. I asked him one day why he thought he was doing so much better than last year. He gave meaning to my whole new orientation. "It's because I like myself now when I'm with you," he said.

A teacher quoted by
Everett Shostrom in
Man, The Manipulator

All The Good Things

He was in the third grade class I taught at Saint Mary's School in Morris, Minnesota. All 34 of my students were dear to me, but Mark Eklund was one in a million. Very neat in appearance, he had that happy-to-be-alive attitude that made even his occasional mischievousness delightful.

Mark also talked incessantly. I tried to remind him again and again that talking without permission was not acceptable. What impressed me so much, though, was the sincere response every time I had to correct him for misbehaving. "Thank you for correcting me, Sister!" I didn't know what to make of it at first but before long I became accustomed to hearing it many times a day.

One morning my patience was growing thin when Mark talked once too often. I made a novice-teacher's mistake. I looked at Mark and said, "If you say one more word, I am going to tape your mouth shut!"

It wasn't ten seconds later when Chuck blurted out, "Mark is talking again." I hadn't asked any of the students to help me watch Mark, but since I had stated the punishment in front of the class, I had to act on it.

I remember the scene as if it had occurred this morning. I walked to my desk, very deliberately opened the drawer and took out a roll of masking tape. Without saying a word, I proceeded to Mark's desk, tore off two pieces of tape and made a big X with them over his mouth. I then returned to the front of the room.

As I glanced at Mark to see how he was doing, he winked at me. That did it! I started laughing. The entire class cheered as I walked back to Mark's desk, removed the tape and shrugged my shoulders. His first words were, "Thank you for correcting me, Sister."

At the end of the year I was asked to teach junior high math. The years flew by, and before I knew it Mark was in my classroom again. He was more handsome than ever and just as polite. Since he had to listen carefully to my instruction in the "new math," he did not talk as much in ninth grade.

One Friday things just didn't feel right. We had worked hard on a new concept all week, and I sensed that the students were growing frustrated with themselves — and edgy with one another. I had to stop this crankiness before it got out of hand. So I asked them to list the names of the other students in the room on two sheets of paper, leaving a space between each name. Then I told them to think of the nicest thing they could say about each of their classmates and write it down.

It took the remainder of the class period to finish the assignment, but as the students left the room, each one handed me their paper. Chuck smiled. Mark said, "Thank you for teaching me, Sister. Have a good weekend."

That Saturday, I wrote down the name of each student on a separate sheet of paper, and I listed what everyone else had said about that individual. On Monday I gave each student his or her list. Some of them ran two pages. Before long, the entire class was smiling. "Really?" I heard whispered. "I never knew that meant anything to anyone!" "I didn't know others liked me so much!"

No one ever mentioned those papers in class again. I never knew if they discussed them after class or with their parents, but it didn't matter. The exercise had accomplished its purpose. The students were happy with themselves and one another again.

That group of students moved on. Several years later, after I had returned from a vacation, my parents met me at the airport. As we were driving home, Mother asked the usual questions about the trip: How the weather was, my experiences in general. There was a slight lull in the conversation. Mother gave Dad a sideways glance and simply said, "Dad?" My father cleared his throat. "The Eklunds called last night," he began.

"Really?" I said. "I haven't heard from them for several years. I wonder how Mark is."

Dad responded quietly. "Mark was killed in Vietnam," he said. "The funeral is tomorrow, and his parents would like it if you could attend." To this day I can still point to the exact spot on I-494 where Dad told me about Mark.

I had never seen a serviceman in a military coffin before. Mark looked so handsome, so mature. All I could think at that moment was, Mark, I would give all the masking tape in the world if only you could talk to me.

The church was packed with Mark's friends. Chuck's sister sang "The Battle Hymn of the Republic." Why did it have to rain on the day of the funeral? It was difficult enough at the graveside. The pastor said the usual prayers and the bugler played taps.

One by one those who loved Mark took a last walk by the coffin and sprinkled it with holy water.

I was the last one to bless the coffin. As I stood there, one of the soldiers who had acted as a pallbearer came up to me. "Were you Mark's math teacher?" he asked. I nodded as I continued to stare at the coffin. "Mark talked about you a lot," he said.

After the funeral most of Mark's former classmates headed to Chuck's farmhouse for lunch. Mark's mother and father were there, obviously waiting for me. "We want to show you something," his father said, taking a wallet out of his pocket. "They found this on Mark when he was killed. We thought you might recognize it."

Opening the billfold, he carefully removed two worn pieces of notebook paper that had obviously been taped, folded and refolded many times. I knew without looking that the papers were the ones on which I had listed all the good things each of Mark's classmates had said about him. "Thank you so much for doing that," Mark's mother said. "As you can see, Mark treasured it."

Mark's classmates started to gather around us. Chuck smiled rather sheepishly and said, "I still have my list. It's in the top drawer of my desk at home." John's wife said, "John asked me to put his in our wedding album." "I have mine too," Marilyn said. "It's in my diary." Then Vicki, another classmate, reached into her pocketbook, took out her wallet and showed her worn and frazzled list to the group. "I carry this with me at all times," Vicki said without batting an eyelash. "I think we all saved our lists."

That's when I finally sat down and cried. I cried for Mark and for all his friends who would never see him again.

Helen P. Mrosla

You Are A Marvel

Each second we live is a new and unique moment of the universe, a moment that will never be again . . . And what do we teach our children? We teach them that two and two make four, and that Paris is the capital of France.

When will we also teach them what they are?

We should say to each of them: Do you know what you are? You are a marvel. You are unique. In all the years that have passed, there has never been another child like you. Your legs, your arms, your clever fingers, the way you move.

You may become a Shakespeare, a Michaelangelo, a Beethoven. You have the capacity for anything. Yes, you are a marvel. And when you grow up, can you then harm another who is, like you, a marvel?

You must work — we must all work — to make the world worthy of its children.

Pablo Casals

All I Ever Really Needed To Know I Learned In Kindergarten

Most of what I really need to know about how to live and what to do and how to be, I learned in kindergarten. Wisdom was not at the top of the graduate mountain, but there in the sandbox at nursery school.

These are the things I learned: Share everything. Play fair. Don't hit people. Put things back where you found them. Clean up your own mess. Don't take things that aren't yours. Say you're sorry when you hurt somebody. Wash your hands before you eat. Flush. Warm cookies and cold milk are good for you. Live a balanced life. Learn some and think some and draw and paint and sing and dance and play and work every day some.

Take a nap every afternoon. When you go out into the world, watch for traffic, hold hands and stick together. Be aware of wonder. Remember the little seed in the plastic cup. The roots go down and the plant goes up and nobody really knows how or why, but we are all like that.

Goldfish and hamsters and white mice and even the little seed in the plastic cup — they all die. So do we.

And then remember the book about Dick and Jane and the first word you learned, the biggest word of all:

LOOK. Everything you need to know is in there somewhere. The Golden Rule and love and basic sanitation. Ecology and politics and sane living.

Think of what a better world it would be if we all — the whole world — had cookies and milk about 3 o'clock every afternoon and then lay down with our blankets for a nap. Or if we had a basic policy in our nations to always put things back where we found them and cleaned up our own messes. And it is still true, no matter how old you are, when you go out into the world, it is better to hold hands and stick together.

Robert Fulghum

We Learn By Doing

Not many years ago I began to play the cello. Most people would say that what I am doing is "learning to play" the cello. But these words carry into our minds the strange idea that there exists two very different processes: (1) learning to play the cello; and (2) playing the cello. They imply that I will do the first until I have completed it, at which point I will stop the first process and begin the second. In short, I will go on "learning to play" until I have "learned to play" and then I will begin to play. Of course, this is nonsense. There are not two processes, but one. We learn to do something by doing it. There is no other way.

John Holt

The Hand

A Thanksgiving Day editorial in the newspaper told of a school teacher who asked her class of first graders to draw a picture of something they were thankful for. She thought of how little these children from poor neighborhoods actually had to be thankful for. But she knew that most of them would draw pictures of turkeys or tables with food. The teacher was taken aback with the picture Douglas handed in . . . a simple childishly drawn hand.

But whose hand? The class was captivated by the abstract image. "I think it must be the hand of God that brings us food," said one child. "A farmer," said another, "because he grows the turkeys." Finally when the others were at work, the teacher bent over Douglas's desk and asked whose hand it was. "It's your hand, Teacher," he mumbled.

She recalled that frequently at recess she had taken Douglas, a scrubby forlorn child by the hand. She often did that with the children. But it meant so much to Douglas. Perhaps this was everyone's Thanksgiving, not for the material things given to us but for the chance, in whatever small way, to give to others.

Source Unknown

The Royal Knights Of Harlem

Within walking distance of my Manhattan apartment, but also light-years away, there is a part of New York called Spanish Harlem. In many ways it is a Third World country. Infant and maternal mortality rates are about the same as in say, Bangladesh, and average male life expectancy is even shorter. These facts it shares with the rest of Harlem, yet here many people are also separated from the more affluent parts of the city by language. When all this is combined with invisibility in the media, the condescension of many teachers and police who work in this Third World country but wouldn't dream of living there, and textbooks that have little to do with their lives, the lesson for kids is clear: They are "less than" people who live only a few blocks away.

At a junior high that rises from a barren patch of concrete playgrounds and metal fences on East 101st Street, Bill Hall teaches the usual English courses, plus English as a second language to students who arrive directly from Puerto Rico, Central and South America, even Pakistan and Hong Kong. Those kids are faced with a new culture, strange rules, a tough neighborhood and parents who may be feeling just as lost as they are. Bill Hall is faced with them.

While looking for an interest to bind one such

group together and help them to learn English at the same time, Bill noticed someone in the neighborhood carrying a chessboard. As a chess player himself, he knew this game crossed many cultural boundaries, so he got permission from a very skeptical principal to start a chess club after school.

Few of the girls came. Never having seen women playing chess, they assumed this game wasn't for them, and without even a female teacher as a role model, those few who did come gradually dropped out. Some of the boys stayed away, too — chess wasn't the kind of game that made you popular in this neighborhood — but about a dozen remained to learn the basics. Their friends made fun of them for staying after school, and some parents felt that chess was a waste of time since it wouldn't help them get a job, but still, they kept coming. Bill was giving these boys something rare in their lives: the wholehearted attention of someone who believed in them.

Gradually, their skills at both chess and English improved. As they got more expert at the game, Bill took them to chess matches in schools outside Spanish Harlem. Because he paid for their subway fares and pizza dinners, no small thing on his teacher's salary, the boys knew he cared. They began to trust this middle-aged white man a little more.

To help them become more independent, Bill asked each boy to captain one event, and to handle all travel and preparation for it. Gradually, even when Bill wasn't around, the boys began to assume responsibility for each other: to coach those who were lagging behind, to share personal problems and to explain to each other's parents why chess wasn't such a waste of time after all. Gradually, too, this new sense of competence carried over into their classrooms and their grades began to improve.

As they became better students and chess players, Bill Hall's dreams for them grew. With a little money supplied by the Manhattan Chess Club, he took them to the State Finals in Syracuse.

What had been twelve disparate, isolated, often passive, shut-down kids had now become a team with their own chosen name: The Royal Knights. After finishing third in their own state, they were eligible for the Junior High School Finals in California.

By now, however, even Bill's own colleagues were giving him reasons why he shouldn't be spending so much time and effort. In real life, these ghetto kids would never "get past New Jersey," as one teacher put it. Why raise funds to fly them across the country and make them more dissatisfied with their lives? Nonetheless, Bill raised money for tickets to California. In that national competition, they finished seventeenth out of 109 teams.

By now chess had become a subject of school interest — if only because it led to trips. On one of their days at a New York chess club, the team members met a young girl from the Soviet Union who was the Women's World Champion. Even Bill was floored by the idea that two of his kids came up with: If this girl could come all the way from Russia, why couldn't The Royal Knights go there? After all, it *was* the chess capital of the world, and the Scholastic Chess Friendship Games were coming up.

Though no U.S. players their age had ever entered these games, officials in Bill's school district rallied round the idea. So did a couple of the corporations he approached for travel money. Of course, no one thought his team could win, but that wasn't the goal. The trip itself would widen the boys' horizons, Bill argued. When Pepsi-Cola came up with a $20,000 check, Bill began to realize that this crazy dream was going to come true.

They boarded the plane for the first leg of their trip to Russia as official representatives of the country from which they had felt so estranged only a few months before. But as veterans of Spanish Harlem, they also made very clear that they were representing their own neighborhood. On the back of their satin athletic jackets was emblazoned not "U.S.A.," but "The Royal Knights."

Once they were in Moscow, however, their confidence began to falter badly. The experience and deliberate style of their Soviet opponents were something they had never previously encountered. Finally one of the Knights broke the spell by playing a Soviet Grand master in his 30s to a draw in a simulation match. The Russians weren't invincible after all; just people like them. After that, the Knights won about half their matches, and even discovered a homegrown advantage in the special event of speed chess. Unlike the Soviet players, who had been taught that slowness and deliberation were virtues, the Knights had a street smart style that made them both fast and accurate.

By the time Bill and his team got to Leningrad to take on the toughest part of their competition, the boys were feeling good again. Though they had been selected at random for their need to learn English, not for any talent at chess, and though they had been playing for only a few months, they won one match and achieved a draw in another.

When the Knights got back to New York, they were convinced they could do anything.

It was a conviction they would need. A few months later when I went to their junior high school club room, Bill Hall, a big gentle man who rarely gets angry, was furious about a recent confrontation between one of the Puerto Rican team members and a white teacher. As Bill urged the boy to explain to me, he had done so well on a test that the teacher, thinking he had cheated, made him take it over. When the boy did well a second time, the teacher seemed less pleased than annoyed to have been proven wrong. "If this had been a school in a different neighborhood," said Bill, "none of this would have happened."

It was the kind of classroom bias that these boys had been internalizing — but now had the self-esteem to resist. "Maybe the teacher was just jealous," the boy said cheerfully. "I mean, we put this school on the map."

And so they had. Their dingy junior high auditorium had just been chosen by a Soviet dance troupe as the site of a New York performance. Every principal in the school district was asking for a chess program, and local television and newspapers had interviewed The Royal Knights. Now that their junior high graduation was just weeks away, bids from various high schools with programs for "gifted" kids were flooding in, even one from a high school in California. Though all the boys were worried about their upcoming separation, it was the other team members who persuaded the boy who got that invitation to accept it.

"We told him to go for it," as one said. "We promised to write him every week," said another. "Actually," said a third, "we all plan to stay in touch for life."

With career plans that included law, accounting, teaching, computer sciences — futures they wouldn't have thought possible before — there was no telling what continuing surprises they might share at reunions of this team that had become its own support group and family.

What were they doing, I asked, *before* Bill Hall and chess playing came into their lives? There was a very long silence.

"Hanging out in the street and feeling like s---," said one boy, who now wants to become a lawyer.

"Taking lunch money from younger kids and a few drugs now and then," admitted another.

"Just lying on my bed, reading comics, and getting yelled at by my father for being lazy," said a third.

Was there anything in their schoolbooks that made a difference?

"Not until Mr. Hall thought we were smart," explained one to the nods of the others, "and then we were."

Gloria Steinem

The Little Boy

Once a little boy went to school.
He was quite a little boy.
And it was quite a big school.
But when the little boy
Found that he could go to his room
By walking right in from the door outside,
He was happy.
And the school did not seem
Quite so big any more.

One morning,
When the little boy had been in school a while,
The teacher said:

"Today we are going to make a picture."
"Good!" thought the little boy.
He liked to make pictures.
He could make all kinds:
Lions and tigers,
Chickens and cows,
Trains and boats —
And he took out his box of crayons
And began to draw.

But the teacher said:
"Wait! It is not time to begin!"
And she waited until everyone looked ready.

"Now," said the teacher,
"We are going to make flowers."
"Good!" thought the little boy,
He liked to make flowers,
And he began to make beautiful ones
With his pink and orange and blue crayons.

But the teacher said,
"Wait! And I will show you how."
And she drew a flower on the blackboard.
It was red, with a green stem.
"There," said the teacher.
"Now you may begin."

The little boy looked at the teacher's flower.
Then he looked at his own flower,
He liked his flower better than the teacher's.
But he did not say this,
He just turned his paper over
And made a flower like the teacher's.
It was red, with a green stem.

On another day,
When the little boy had opened
The door from the outside all by himself,
The teacher said,
"Today we are going to make something with clay."
"Good!" thought the little boy.
He liked clay.

He could make all kinds of things with clay:
Snakes and snowmen,
Elephants and mice,

Cars and trucks —
And he began to pull and pinch
His ball of clay.

But the teacher said,
"Wait! It is not time to begin!"
And she waited until everyone looked ready.

"Now," said the teacher,
"We are going to make a dish."
"Good!" thought the little boy,
He liked to make dishes,
And he began to make some
That were all shapes and sizes.

But the teacher said,
"Wait! And I will show you how."
And she showed everyone how to make
One deep dish.
"There," said the teacher,
"Now you may begin."

The little boy looked at the teacher's dish
Then he looked at his own.
He liked his dishes better than the teacher's
But he did not say this,
He just rolled his clay into a big ball again,
And made a dish like the teacher's.
It was a deep dish.

And pretty soon
The little boy learned to wait
And to watch,
And to make things just like the teacher.
And pretty soon
He didn't make things of his own anymore.

Then it happened
That the little boy and his family
Moved to another house,
In another city,
And the little boy
Had to go to another school.

This school was even Bigger
Than the other one,
And there was no door from the outside
Into his room.
He had to go up some big steps,
And walk down a long hall
To get to his room.

And the very first day
He was there, the teacher said,
"Today we are going to make a picture."

"Good!" thought the little boy,
And he waited for the teacher
To tell him what to do
But the teacher didn't say anything.
She just walked around the room.

When she came to the little boy,
She said, "Don't you want to make a picture?"
"Yes," said the little boy.
"What are we going to make?"
"I don't know until you make it," said the teacher.
"How shall I make it?" asked the little boy.
"Why, any way you like," said the teacher.
"And any color?" asked the little boy.
"Any color," said the teacher,
"If everyone made the same picture,
And used the same colors,
How would I know who made what,

And which was which?"
"I don't know," said the little boy.
And he began to make pink and orange
and blue flowers.

He liked his new school,
Even if it didn't have a door
Right in from the outside!

Helen E. Buckley

I Am A Teacher

I am a Teacher.
I was born the first moment that a question leaped from the mouth of a child.
I have been many people in many places.
I am Socrates exciting the youth of Athens to discover new ideas through the use of questions.
I am Anne Sullivan tapping out the secrets of the universe into the outstretched hand of Helen Keller.
I am Aesop and Hans Christian Andersen revealing truth through countless stories.
I am Marva Collins fighting for every child's right to an education.
I am Mary McCleod Bethune building a great college for my people, using orange crates for desks.
And I am Bel Kaufman struggling to go *Up The Down Staircase.*
The names of those who have practiced my profession ring like a hall of fame for humanity . . . Booker T. Washington, Buddha, Confucious, Ralph Waldo Emerson, Leo Buscaglia, Moses and Jesus.
I am also those whose names and faces have long been forgotten but whose lessons and character will always be remembered in the accomplishments of their students.

I have wept for joy at the weddings of former students, laughed with glee at the birth of their children and stood with head bowed in grief and confusion by graves dug too soon for bodies far too young.

Throughout the course of a day I have been called upon to be an actor, friend, nurse and doctor, coach, finder of lost articles, money lender, taxi driver, psychologist, substitute parent, salesman, politician and a keeper of the faith.

Despite the maps, charts, formulas, verbs, stories and books, I have really had nothing to teach, for my students really have only themselves to learn, and I know it takes the whole world to tell you who you are.

I am a paradox. I speak loudest when I listen the most. My greatest gifts are in what I am willing to appreciatively receive from my students.

Material wealth is not one of my goals, but I am a full-time treasure seeker in my quest for new opportunities for my students to use their talents and in my constant search for those talents that sometimes lie buried in self-defeat.

I am the most fortunate of all who labor.

A doctor is allowed to usher life into the world in one magic moment. I am allowed to see that life is reborn each day with new questions, ideas and friendships.

An architect knows that if he builds with care, his structure may stand for centuries. A teacher knows that if he builds with love and truth, what he builds will last forever.

I am a warrior, daily doing battle against peer pressure, negativity, fear, conformity, prejudice, ignorance and apathy. But I have great allies: Intelligence, Curiosity, Parental Support, Individuality, Creativity, Faith,

Love and Laughter all rush to my banner with indomitable support.

And who do I have to thank for this wonderful life I am so fortunate to experience, but you the public, the parents. For you have done me the great honor to entrust to me your greatest contribution to eternity, your children.

And so I have a past that is rich in memories. I have a present that is challenging, adventurous and fun because I am allowed to spend my days with the future.

I am a teacher . . . and I thank God for it every day.

John W. Schlatter

5

LIVE YOUR DREAM

People who say it cannot be done should not interrupt those who are doing it.

I Think I Can!

Whether you think you can or think you can't, you're right.

Henry Ford

Rocky Lyons, the son of New York Jets defensive end Marty Lyons, was five years old when he was driving through rural Alabama with his mother, Kelly. He was asleep on the front seat of their pickup truck, with his feet resting on her lap.

As his mom drove carefully down the winding two-lane country road, she turned onto a narrow bridge. As she did, the truck hit a pothole and slid off the road, and the right front wheel got stuck in a rut. Fearing the truck would tip over, she attempted to jerk it back up onto the road by pressing hard on the gas pedal and spinning the steering wheel to the left. But Rocky's foot got caught between her leg and the steering wheel and she lost control of the pickup truck.

The truck flipped over and over down a 20-foot ravine. When it hit bottom, Rocky woke up. "What happened, Mama?" he asked. "Our wheels are pointing toward the sky."

Kelly was blinded by blood. The gearshift had jammed into her face, ripping it open from lip to forehead. Her gums were torn out, her cheeks pulverized, her shoulders crushed. With one shattered bone sticking out of her armpit, she was pinned against the crushed door.

"I'll get you out, Mama," announced Rocky, who had miraculously escaped injury. He slithered out from under Kelly, slid through the open window and tried to yank his mother out. But she didn't move. "Just let me sleep," begged Kelly, who was drifting in and out of consciousness. "No, Mama," Rocky insisted. "You can't go to sleep."

Rocky wriggled back into the truck and managed to push Kelly out of the wreckage. He then told her he'd climb up to the road and stop a car to get help. Fearing that no one would be able to see her little boy in the dark, Kelly refused to let him go alone. Instead they slowly crept up the embankment, with Rocky using his meager 40-pound frame to push his 104-pound mother. They crawled inches at a time. The pain was so great that Kelly wanted to give up, but Rocky wouldn't let her.

To urge his mother on, Rocky told her to think "about that little train," the one in the classic children's story, *The Little Engine That Could,* which managed to get up a steep mountain. To remind her, Rocky kept repeating his version of the story's inspirational phrase: "I know you can, I know you can."

When they finally reached the road, Rocky was able to see his mother's torn face clearly for the first time. He broke into tears. Waving his arms and pleading, "Stop! Please stop!" the boy hailed a truck. "Get my mama to a hospital," he implored the driver.

It took 8 hours and 344 stitches to rebuild Kelly's face. She looks quite different today — "I used to have a straight long nose, thin lips and high cheekbones; now I've got a pug nose, flat cheeks and much bigger lips" — but she has few visible scars and has recovered from her injuries.

Rocky's heroics were big news. But the spunky youngster insists he didn't do anything extraordinary. "It's not like I wanted it to happen," he explains. "I just did what anyone would have done." Says his mother, "If it weren't for Rocky, I'd have bled to death."

First heard from
Michele Borba

Rest In Peace: The "I Can't" Funeral

Donna's fourth-grade classroom looked like many others I had seen in the past. Students sat in five rows of six desks. The teacher's desk was in the front and faced the students. The bulletin board featured student work. In most respects it appeared to be a typically traditional elementary classroom. Yet something seemed different that day I entered it for the first time. There seemed to be an undercurrent of excitement.

Donna was a veteran small-town Michigan school-teacher only two years away from retirement. In addition she was a volunteer participant in a county-wide staff development project I had organized and facilitated. The training focused on language arts ideas that would empower students to feel good about themselves and take charge of their lives. Donna's job was to attend training sessions and implement the concepts being presented. My job was to make classroom visitations and encourage implementation.

I took an empty seat in the back of the room and watched. All the students were working on a task, filling a sheet of notebook paper with thoughts and ideas. The ten-year-old student closest to me was filling her page with "I Can'ts."

"I can't kick the soccer ball past second base."

"I can't do long division with more than three numerals."

"I can't get Debbie to like me."

Her page was half full and she showed no signs of letting up. She worked on with determination and persistence.

I walked down the row glancing at students' papers. Everyone was writing sentences, describing things they couldn't do.

"I can't do ten push-ups."

"I can't hit one over the left-field fence."

"I can't eat only one cookie."

By this time, the activity engaged my curiosity, so I decided to check with the teacher to see what was going on. As I approached her, I noticed that she too was busy writing. I felt it best not to interrupt.

"I can't get John's mother to come in for a teacher conference."

"I can't get my daughter to put gas in the car."

"I can't get Alan to use words instead of fists."

Thwarted in my efforts to determine why students and teacher were dwelling on the negative instead of writing the more positive "I Can" statements, I returned to my seat and continued my observations. Students wrote for another ten minutes. Most filled their page. Some started another.

"Finish the one you're on and don't start a new one," were the instructions Donna used to signal the end of the activity. Students were then instructed to fold their papers in half and bring them to the front. When students reached the teacher's desk, they placed their "I Can't" statements into an empty shoe box.

When all of the student papers were collected, Donna added hers. She put the lid on the box, tucked it under her arm and headed out the door and down the hall. Students followed the teacher. I followed the students.

Halfway down the hall the procession stopped. Donna entered the custodian's room, rummaged around and came out with a shovel. Shovel in one hand, shoe box in the other, Donna marched the students out of the school to the farthest corner of the playground. There they began to dig.

They were going to bury their "I Can'ts"! The digging took over ten minutes because most of the fourth graders wanted a turn. When the hole approached three-feet deep, the digging ended. The box of "I Can'ts" was placed in position at the bottom of the hole and quickly covered with dirt.

Thirty-one 10- and 11-year-olds stood around the freshly dug grave site. Each had at least one page full of "I Can'ts" in the shoe box, four-feet under. So did their teacher.

At this point Donna announced, "Boys and girls, please join hands and bow your heads." The students complied. They quickly formed a circle around the grave, creating a bond with their hands. They lowered their heads and waited. Donna delivered the eulogy.

"Friends, we gather today to honor the memory of 'I Can't.' While he was with us on earth, he touched the lives of everyone, some more than others. His name, unfortunately, has been spoken in every public building — schools, city halls, state capitols and yes, even The White House.

"We have provided 'I Can't' with a final resting place and a headstone that contains his epitaph. He is survived by his brothers and sister, 'I Can', 'I Will' and 'I'm Going to Right Away.' They are not as well known as their famous relative and are certainly not as strong and powerful yet. Perhaps some day, with your help, they will make an even bigger mark on the world.

"May 'I Can't' rest in peace and may everyone present pick up their lives and move forward in his absence. Amen."

As I listened to the eulogy I realized that these students would never forget this day. The activity was symbolic, a metaphor for life. It was a right-brain experience that would stick in the unconscious and conscious mind forever.

Writing "I Can'ts," burying them and hearing the eulogy. That was a major effort on the part of this teacher. And she wasn't done yet. At the conclusion of the eulogy she turned the students around, marched them back into the classroom and held a wake.

They celebrated the passing of "I Can't" with cookies, popcorn and fruit juices. As part of the celebration, Donna cut out a large tombstone from butcher paper. She wrote the words "I Can't" at the top and put RIP in the middle. The date was added at the bottom.

The paper tombstone hung in Donna's classroom for the remainder of the year. On those rare occasions when a student forgot and said, "I Can't," Donna simply pointed to the RIP sign. The student then remembered that "I Can't" was dead and chose to rephrase the statement.

I wasn't one of Donna's students. She was one of mine. Yet that day I learned an enduring lesson from her.

Now, years later, whenever I hear the phrase, "I Can't," I see images of that fourth-grade funeral. Like the students, I remember that "I Can't" is dead.

Chick Moorman

The 333 Story

I was doing a weekend seminar at the Deerhurst Lodge, north of Toronto. On Friday night a tornado swept through a town north of us called Barrie, killing dozens of people and doing millions of dollars worth of damage. Sunday night, as I was coming home, I stopped the car when I got to Barrie. I got out on the side of the highway and looked around. It was a mess. Everywhere I looked there were smashed houses and cars turned upside down.

That same night Bob Templeton was driving down the same highway. He stopped to look at the disaster just as I had, only his thoughts were different than my own. Bob was the vice-president of Telemedia Communications, which owns a string of radio stations in Ontario and Quebec. He thought there must be something we could do for these people with the radio stations they had.

The following night I was doing another seminar in Toronto. Bob Templeton and Bob Johnson, another vice-president from Telemedia, came in and stood in the back of the room. They shared their conviction that there had to be something they could do for the people in Barrie. After the seminar we went back to Bob's office. He was now committed to the idea of helping the people who had been caught in the tornado.

The following Friday he called all the executives at Telemedia into his office. At the top of a flip chart he wrote three 3s. He said to his executives "How would you like to raise 3 million dollars 3 days from now in just 3 hours and give the money to the people in Barrie?" There was nothing but silence in the room.

Finally someone said, "Templeton, you're crazy. There is no way we could do that."

Bob said, "Wait a minute. I didn't ask you if we *could* or even if we *should.* I just asked you if you'd like to."

They all said, "Sure, we'd *like* to." He then drew a large T underneath the 333. On one side he wrote, "Why we can't." On the other side he wrote, "How we can."

"I'm going to put a big X on the 'Why we can't side.' We're not going to spend any time on the ideas of why we can't. That's of no value. On the other side we're going to write down every idea that we can come up with on how we can. We're not going to leave the room until we figure it out." There was silence again.

Finally, someone said, "We could do a radio show across Canada."

Bob said, "That's a great idea," and wrote it down.

Before he had it written, someone said, "You can't do a radio show across Canada. We don't have radio stations across Canada." That was a pretty valid objection. They only had stations in Ontario and Quebec.

Templeton replied, "That's why we can. That stays." But this was a really strong objection because radio stations are very competitive. They usually don't work together and to get them to do so would be virtually impossible according to the standard way of thinking.

All of a sudden someone suggested, "You could get Harvey Kirk and Lloyd Robertson, the biggest names in Canadian broadcasting, to anchor the show." (That would be like getting Tom Brokaw and Sam Donaldson to anchor the show. They are anchors on national TV. They are not going to go on radio.) At that point it was absolutely amazing how fast and furious the creative ideas began to flow.

That was on a Friday. The following Tuesday they had a radiothon. They had 50 radio stations all across the country that agreed to broadcast it. It didn't matter who got the credit as long as the people in Barrie got the money. Harvey Kirk and Lloyd Robertson anchored the show and they succeeded in raising 3 million dollars in 3 hours within 3 business days!

You see, you can do anything if you put your focus on how to do it rather than on why you can't.

Bob Proctor

There Are No Vans

I remember one Thanksgiving when our family had no money and no food, and someone came knocking on our door. A man was standing there with a huge box of food, a giant turkey and even some pans to cook it in. I couldn't believe it. My dad demanded, "Who are you? Where are you from?"

The stranger announced, "I'm here because a friend of yours knows you're in need and that you wouldn't accept direct help, so I've brought this for you. Have a great Thanksgiving."

My father said, "No, no, we can't accept this." The stranger replied "You don't have a choice," closed the door and left.

Obviously that experience had a profound impact on my life. I promised myself that someday I would do well enough financially so that I could do the same thing for other people. By the time I was 18 I had created my Thanksgiving ritual. I like to do things spontaneously, so I would go out shopping and buy enough food for one or two families. Then I would dress like a delivery boy, go to the poorest neighborhood and just knock on a door. I always included a note that explained my Thanksgiving experience as a kid. The note concluded, "All that I ask in return is that you take good enough care of yourself so that someday you can do the same thing for someone else." I have received more from this annual ritual than I have from any amount of money I've ever earned.

Several years ago I was in New York City with my new wife during Thanksgiving. She was sad because we were not with our family. Normally she would be home decorating the house for Christmas, but we were stuck here in a hotel room.

I said, "Honey, look, why don't we decorate some lives today instead of some old trees?" When I told her what I always do on Thanksgiving, she got excited. I said, "Let's go someplace where we can really appreciate who we are, what we are capable of and what we can really give. Let's go to Harlem!" She and several of my business partners who were with us weren't really enthusiastic about the idea. I urged them: "C'mon, let's go to Harlem and feed some people in need. We won't be the people who are giving it because that would be insulting. We'll just be the delivery people. We'll go buy enough food for six or seven families for 30 days. We've got enough. Let's just go do it! That's what Thanksgiving really is: Giving good thanks, not eating turkey. C'mon. Let's go do it!"

Because I had to do a radio interview first, I asked my partners to get us started by getting a van. When I returned from the interview, they said "We just can't do it. There are no vans in all of New York. The rent-a-car places are all out of vans. They're just not available."

I said, "Look, the bottom line is that if we want something, we can make it happen! All we have to do is take action. There are plenty of vans here in New York City. We just don't have one. Let's go get one."

They insisted, "We've called everywhere. There aren't any."

I said, "Look down at the street. Look down there. Do you see all those vans?" They said, "Yeah, we see them."

"Let's go get one," I said. First I tried walking out in front of vans as they were driving down the street. I learned something about New York drivers that day: They don't stop; they speed up.

Then we tried waiting by the light. We'd go over and knock on the window and the driver would roll it down, looking at us kind of leery, and I'd say, "Hi. Since today is Thanksgiving, we'd like to know if you would be willing to drive us to Harlem so we can feed some people." Every time the driver would look away quickly, furiously roll up the window and pull away without saying anything.

Eventually we got better at asking. We'd knock on the window, they'd roll it down and we'd say, "Today is Thanksgiving. We'd like to help some underprivileged people, and we're curious if you'd be willing to drive us to an underprivileged area that we have in mind here in New York City." That seemed slightly more effective but still didn't work. Then we started offering people $100 to drive us. That got us even closer, but when we told them to take us to Harlem, they said no and drove off.

We had talked to about two dozen people who all said no. My partners were ready to give up on the project, but I said, "It's the law of averages: somebody is going to say *yes*." Sure enough, the perfect van drove up. It was perfect because it was extra big and would accomodate all of us. We went up, knocked on the window and we asked the driver, "Could you take us to a disadvantaged area? We'll pay you a hundred dollars."

The driver said, "You don't have to pay me. I'd be happy to take you. In fact, I'll take you to some of the most difficult spots in the whole city." Then he reached over on the seat and grabbed his hat. As he put it on, I noticed that it said, "Salvation Army." The man's name was Captain John Rondon and he was the head of the Salvation Army in the South Bronx.

We climbed into the van in absolute ecstasy. He said, "I'll take you places you never even thought of going. But tell me something. Why do you people want to do this?" I told him my story and that I wanted to show gratitude for all that I had by giving something back.

Captain Rondon took us into parts of the South Bronx that make Harlem look like Beverly Hills. When we arrived, we went into a store where we bought a lot of food and some baskets. We packed enough for seven families for 30 days. Then we went out to start feeding people. We went to buildings where there were half a dozen people living in one room: "squatters" with no electricity and no heat in the dead of winter surrounded by rats, cockroaches and the smell of urine. It was both an astonishing realization that people lived this way and a truly fulfilling experience to make even a small difference.

You see, you can make anything happen if you commit to it and take action. Miracles like this happen every day — even in a city where "there are no vans."

Anthony Robbins

Ask, Ask, Ask

The greatest saleswoman in the world today doesn't mind if you call her a girl. That's because Markita Andrews has generated more than eighty thousand dollars selling Girl Scout cookies since she was seven years old.

Going door-to-door after school, the painfully shy Markita transformed herself into a cookie-selling dynamo when she discovered, at age 13, the secret of selling.

It starts with desire. Burning, white-hot desire.

For Markita and her mother, who worked as a waitress in New York after her husband left them when Markita was eight years old, their dream was to travel the globe. "I'll work hard to make enough money to send you to college," her mother said one day. "You'll go to college and when you graduate, you'll make enough money to take you and me around the world. Okay?"

So at age 13 when Markita read in her Girl Scout magazine that the Scout who sold the most cookies would win an all-expenses-paid trip for two around the world, she decided to sell all the Girl Scout cookies she could — more Girl Scout cookies than anyone in the world, ever.

But desire alone is not enough. To make her dream come true, Markita knew she needed a plan.

"Always wear your right outfit, your professional garb," her aunt advised. "When you are doing business, dress like you are doing business. Wear your Girl Scout uniform. When you go up to people in their tenement buildings at 4:30 or 6:30 and especially on Friday night, ask for a big order. Always smile, whether they buy or not, always be nice. And don't ask them to buy your cookies; ask them to invest."

Lots of other Scouts may have wanted that trip around the world. Lots of other Scouts may have had a plan. But only Markita went off in her uniform each day after school, ready to ask — and keep asking — folks to invest in her dream. "Hi. I have a dream. I'm earning a trip around the world for me and my mom by merchandising Girl Scout cookies," she'd say at the door. "Would you like to invest in one dozen or two dozen boxes of cookies?"

Markita sold 3,526 boxes of Girl Scout cookies that year and won her trip around the world. Since then, she has sold more than 42,000 boxes of Girl Scout cookies, spoken at sales conventions across the country, starred in a Disney movie about her adventure and has co-authored the best seller, *How to Sell More Cookies, Condos, Cadillacs, Computers . . . And Everything Else.*

Markita is no smarter and no more extroverted than thousands of other people, young and old, with dreams of their own. The difference is Markita has discovered the secret of selling: Ask, Ask, Ask! Many people fail before they even begin because they fail to *ask* for what they want. The fear of rejection leads many of us to reject ourselves and our dreams long before anyone else ever has the chance — no matter what we're selling.

And everyone is selling something. "You're selling yourself everyday — in school, to your boss, to new people you meet," said Markita at 14. "My mother is a waitress: she sells the daily special. Mayors and presidents trying to get votes are selling . . . One of my favorite teachers was Mrs. Chapin. She made geography interesting, and that's really selling . . . I see selling everywhere I look. Selling is part of the whole world."

It takes courage to ask for what you want. Courage is not the absence of fear. It's doing what it takes despite one's fear. And, as Markita has discovered, the more you ask, the easier (and more fun) it gets.

Once, on live TV, the producer decided to give Markita her toughest selling challenge. Markita was asked to sell Girl Scout cookies to another guest on the show. "Would you like to invest in one dozen or two dozen boxes of Girl Scout cookies?" she asked.

"Girl Scout cookies?! I don't buy any Girl Scout cookies!" he replied. "I'm a Federal Penitentiary warden. I put 2,000 rapists, robbers, criminals, muggers and child abusers to bed every night."

Unruffled, Markita quickly countered, "Mister, if you take some of these cookies, maybe you won't be so mean and angry and evil. And, Mister, I think it would be a good idea for you to take some of these cookies back for every one of your 2,000 prisoners, too."

Markita asked.

The Warden wrote a check.

Jack Canfield and Mark V. Hansen

Did The Earth Move For You?

Eleven-year-old Angela was stricken with a debilitating disease involving her nervous system. She was unable to walk and her movement was restricted in other ways as well. The doctors did not hold out much hope of her ever recovering from this illness. They predicted she'd spend the rest of her life in a wheelchair. They said that few, if any, were able to come back to normal after contracting this disease. The little girl was undaunted. There, lying in her hospital bed, she would vow to anyone who'd listen that she was definitely going to be walking again someday.

She was transferred to a specialized rehabilitation hospital in the San Francisco Bay area. Whatever therapies could be applied to her case were used. The therapists were charmed by her undefeatable spirit. They taught her about *imaging* — about seeing herself walking. If it would do nothing else, it would at least give her hope and something positive to do in the long waking hours in her bed. Angela would work as hard as possible in physical therapy, in whirlpools and in exercise sessions. But she worked just as hard lying there faithfully doing her imaging, visualizing herself moving, moving, moving!

One day, as she was straining with all her might to imagine her legs moving again, it seemed as though a miracle happened: The bed moved! It began to move around the room! She screamed out, "Look what I'm doing! Look! Look! I can do it! I moved, *I moved!*"

Of course, at this very moment everyone else in the hospital was screaming, too, and running for cover. People were screaming, equipment was falling and glass was breaking. You see, it was the recent San Francisco earthquake. But don't tell that to Angela. She's convinced that she did it. And now only a few years later, she's back in school. On her own two legs. No crutches, no wheelchair. You see, anyone who can shake the earth between San Francisco and Oakland can conquer a piddling little disease, can't they?

Hanoch McCarty

Tommy's Bumper Sticker

A little kid down at our church in Huntington Beach came up to me after he heard me talk about the Children's Bank. He shook my hand and said, "My name is Tommy Tighe, I'm six years old and I want to borrow money from your Children's Bank."

I said, "Tommy, that's one of my goals, to loan money to kids. And so far all the kids have paid it back. What do you want to do?"

He said, "Ever since I was four I had a vision that I could cause peace in the world. I want to make a bumper sticker that says, 'PEACE, PLEASE! DO IT FOR US KIDS,' signed 'Tommy'. "

"I can get behind that," I said. He needed $454 to produce 1,000 bumper stickers. The Mark Victor Hansen Children's Free Enterprise Fund wrote a check to the printer who was printing the bumper stickers.

Tommy's dad whispered in my ear, "If he doesn't pay the loan back, are you going to foreclose on his bicycle?"

I said, "No, knock on wood, every kid is born with honesty, morality and ethics. They have to be taught something else. I believe he'll pay us back." If you have a child who is over nine, let them w-o-r-k for m-o-n-e-y for someone honest, moral and ethical so they learn the principle early.

We gave Tommy a copy of all of my tapes and he listened to them 21 times each and took ownership of the material. It says, "Always start selling at the top." Tommy convinced his dad to drive him up to Ronald Reagan's home. Tommy rang the bell and the gatekeeper came out. Tommy gave a two-minute, irresistible sales presentation on his bumper sticker. The gatekeeper reached in his pocket, gave Tommy $1.50 and said, "Here, I want one of those. Hold on and I'll get the former President."

I asked, "Why did you ask him to buy?" He said, "You said in the tapes to ask everyone to buy." I said, "I did. I did. I'm guilty."

He sent a bumper sticker to Mikhail Gorbachev with a bill for $1.50 in U.S. funds. Gorbachev sent him back $1.50 and a picture that said, "Go for peace, Tommy," and signed it, "Mikhail Gorbachev, President."

Since I collect autographs, I told Tommy, "I'll give you $500.00 for Gorbachev's autograph."

He said, "No thanks, Mark."

I said, "Tommy, I own several companies. When you get older, I'd like to hire you."

"Are you kidding?" he answered. "When I get older, I'm going to hire you."

The Sunday edition of the *Orange County Register* did a feature section on Tommy's story, the Children's Free Enterprise Bank and me. Marty Shaw, the journalist, interviewed Tommy for six hours and wrote a phenomenal interview. Marty asked Tommy what he thought his impact would be on world peace. Tommy said, "I don't think I am old enough yet; I think you have to be eight or nine to stop all the wars in the world."

Marty asked, "Who are your heroes?"

He said, "My dad, George Burns, Wally Joiner and Mark Victor Hansen." Tommy has good taste in role models.

Three days later, I got a call from the Hallmark Greeting Card Company. A Hallmark franchisee had faxed a copy of the *Register* article. They were having a convention in San Francisco and wanted Tommy to speak. After all, they saw that Tommy had nine goals for himself:

1. Call about cost (baseball card collateral).
2. Have bumper sticker printed.
3. Make a plan for a loan.
4. Find out how to tell people.
5. Get address of leaders.
6. Write a letter to all of the presidents and leaders of other countries and send them all a free bumper sticker.
7. Talk to everyone about peace.
8. Call the newspaper stand and talk about my business.
9. Have a talk with school.

Hallmark wanted my company, Look Who's Talking, to book Tommy to speak. While the talk did not happen because the two-week lead time was too short, the negotiation between Hallmark, myself and Tommy was fun, uplifting and powerful.

Joan Rivers called Tommy Tighe to be on her syndicated television show. Someone had also faxed her a copy of the *Register* interview on Tommy.

"Tommy," Joan said, "this is Joan Rivers and I want you on my TV show which is viewed by millions."

"Great!" said Tommy. He didn't know her from a bottle of Vicks.

"I'll pay you $300," said Joan.

"Great!" said Tommy. Having listened repeatedly to and mastered my *Sell Yourself Rich* tapes, Tommy continued selling Joan by saying: "I am only eight years old, so I can't come alone. You can afford to pay for my mom, too, can't you, Joan?"

"Yes!" Joan replied.

"By the way, I just watched a *Lifestyles of the Rich and Famous* show and it said to stay at the Trump Plaza when you're in New York. You can make that happen, can't you, Joan?"

"Yes," she answered.

"The show also said when in New York, you ought to visit the Empire State Building and the Statue of Liberty. You can get us tickets, can't you?"

"Yes . . ."

"Great. Did I tell you my mom doesn't drive? So we can use your limo, can't we?"

"Sure," said Joan.

Tommy went on *The Joan Rivers Show* and wowed Joan, the camera crew, the live and television audiences. He was so handsome, interesting, authentic and such a great self-starter. He told such captivating and persuasive stories that the audience was found pulling money out of their wallets to buy a bumper sticker on the spot.

At the end of the show, Joan leaned in and asked, "Tommy, do you really think your bumper sticker will cause peace in the world?"

Tommy, enthusiastically and with a radiant smile, said, "So far I've had it out two years and got the Berlin Wall down. I'm doing pretty good, don't you think?"

Mark V. Hansen

*To date Tommy has sold over 2,500 of his bumper stickers and has repaid his $454 loan to Mark Victor Hansen's Children's Free Enterprise Bank. If you'd like to order one of Tommy's bumper stickers, send $3.00 to Tommy Tighe, 17283 Ward Street, Fountain Valley, CA 92708.

If You Don't Ask, You Don't Get — But If You Do, You Do

My wife Linda and I live in Miami, Florida. When we had just started our self-esteem training program called Little Acorns to teach children how to say no to drugs, sexual promiscuity and other self-destructive behavior, we received a brochure for an educational conference in San Diego. As we read the brochure and realized that everybody who is anybody was going to be there, we realized we had to go. But we didn't see how. We were just getting started, we were working out of our home and had just about exhausted our personal savings with the early stages of the work. There was no way we could afford the airline tickets or any of the other expenses. But we knew we had to be there, so we started asking.

The first thing I did was to call the conference coordinators in San Diego, explain why we just had to be there and ask them if they would give us two complimentary admissions to the conference. When I explained our situation, what we were doing and why we had to be there, they said yes. So now we had the tickets.

I told Linda we had the tickets and we could get into the conference. She said, "Great! But we're in

Miami and the conference is in San Diego. What do we do next?"

So I said, "We've got to get transportation." I called an airline I knew was doing well at the time, Northeast Airlines. The woman who answered happened to be the secretary to the president so I told her what I needed. She put me directly through to the president, Steve Quinto. I explained to him that I had just talked to the conference people in San Diego, they had given us free tickets to the conference but we were stuck on how to get there and would he please donate two roundtrip tickets from Miami to San Diego. He said, "Of course I will," just like that. It was that fast and the next thing he said really floored me. He said, "Thank you for asking."

I said, "Pardon me?"

He said "I don't often have the opportunity to do the best thing that I can for the world unless someone asks me to. The best thing I can ever do is to give of myself and you've asked me to do that. That's a nice opportunity and I want to thank you for that opportunity." I was blown away, but I thanked him and hung up the phone. I looked at my wife and said, "Honey, we got the plane tickets." She said, "Great! Where do we stay?"

Next I called the Holiday Inn Downtown Miami and asked, "Where is your headquarters?" They told me it was in Memphis, Tennessee, so I called Tennessee and they patched me through to the person I needed to talk to. It was a guy in San Francisco. He controlled all of the Holiday Inns in California. I then explained to him that we had obtained our plane tickets through the airlines and asked if there were some way he could help us with the lodging for the three days. He asked if it would be okay if he put us up in their new hotel in downtown San Diego as his guest. I said, "Yes, that would be fine."

He then said, "Wait a minute. I need to caution you that the hotel is about a 35-mile drive from the campus where the conference is being held and you'll have to find out how to get there."

I said, "I'll figure it out if I need to buy a horse." I thanked him and I said to Linda, "Well, honey, we've got the admission, we've got the plane tickets and we've got a place to stay. What we need now is a way to get back and forth from the hotel to the campus twice a day.

Next I called National Car Rental, told them the story and asked if they could help me out. They said, "Would a new Olds 88 be okay?" I said it would be.

In one day we had put the whole thing together.

We did wind up buying our own meals for part of the time but before the conference was over, I stood up, told this story at one of the general assemblies and said, "Anyone who wants to volunteer to take us to lunch now and again would be graciously thanked." About fifty people jumped up and volunteered so we wound up having some of the meals thrown in as well.

We had a marvelous time, learned a lot and connected with people like Jack Canfield who is still on our advisory board. When we returned, we launched the program and it's been growing about 100 percent a year. This last June we graduated our 2,250th family from the Little Acorn training. We've also held two major conferences for educators called *Making The World Safe For Children,* to which we've invited people from all over the world. Thousands of educators have come to get ideas on how to do self-esteem training in their classrooms while they're still teaching the three Rs.

The last time we sponsored the conference we invited educators from 81 nations to come. Seventeen nations sent representatives including some ministers of education. Out of that has grown invitations for us to take our program to the following places: Russia, Ukraine, Byelorussia, Gelaruth, Kazakhstan, Mongolia, Taiwan, the Cook Islands and New Zealand.

So you see you can get anything you want if you just ask enough people.

Rick Gelinas

Rick Little's Quest

At 5 A.M. Rick Little fell asleep at the wheel of his car, hurtled over a ten-foot embankment and crashed into a tree. He spent the next six months in traction with a broken back. Rick found himself with a lot of time to think deeply about his life — something for which the thirteen years of his education had not prepared him. Only two weeks after he was dismissed from the hospital, he returned home one afternoon to find his mother lying semiconscious on the floor from an overdose of sleeping pills. Rick confronted once again the inadequacy of his formal education in preparing him to deal with the social and emotional issues of his life.

During the following months Rick began to formulate an idea — the development of a course that would equip students with high self-esteem, relationship skills and conflict management skills. As Rick began to research what such a course should contain, he ran across a study by the National Institute of Education in which 1,000 30-year-olds had been asked if they felt their high school education had equipped them with the skills they needed for the real world. Over 80 percent responded, "Absolutely not."

These 30-year-olds were also asked what skills they now wish they had been taught. The top answers were relationship skills: How to get along better with the people you live with. How to find and keep a job. How to handle conflict. How to be a good parent. How to understand the normal development of a child. How to handle financial management. And how to intuit the meaning of life.

Inspired by his vision of creating a class that might teach these things, Rick dropped out of college and set across the country to interview high school students. In his quest for information on what should be included in the course, he asked over 2,000 students in 120 high schools the same two questions:

1. If you were to develop a program for your high school to help you cope with what you're meeting now and what you think you'll be meeting in the future, what would that program include?
2. List the top ten problems in your life that you wish were dealt with better at home and in school.

Whether the students were from wealthy private schools or inner city ghettos, rural or suburban, the answers were surprisingly the same. Loneliness and not liking themselves topped the list of problems. In addition, they had the same list of skills they wished they were taught as the ones compiled by the 30-year-olds.

Rick slept in his car for two months, living on a total of $60.00. Most days he ate peanut butter on crackers. Some days he didn't eat at all. Rick had few resources but he was committed to his dream.

His next step was to make a list of the nation's top educators and leaders in counseling and psychology. He set out to visit everyone on his list to ask for their expertise and support. While they were impressed with his approach — asking students directly what they wanted to learn — they offered little help. "You're too young. Go back to college. Get your degree. Go to graduate school, then you can pursue this." They were less than encouraging.

Yet Rick persisted. By the time he turned 20, he had sold his car, his clothes, had borrowed from friends and was $32,000 in debt. Someone suggested he go to a foundation and ask for money.

His first appointment at a local foundation was a huge disappointment. As he walked into the office, Rick was literally shaking with fear. The vice-president of the foundation was a huge dark-haired man with a cold stern face. For a half hour he sat without uttering a word while Rick poured his heart out about his mother, the two thousand kids and plans for a new kind of course for high school kids.

When he was through, the vice-president pushed up a stack of folders. "Son," he said, "I've been here nearly 20 years. We've funded all these education programs. And they all failed. Yours will, too. The reasons? They're obvious. You're 20 years old, you have no experience, no money, no college degree. Nothing!"

As he left the foundation office, Rick vowed to prove this man wrong. Rick began a study of which foundations were interested in funding projects for teenagers. He then spent months writing grant proposals — working from early morning until late at night. Rick worked for over a year laboriously writing grant proposals, each one carefully tailored to the interests and requirements of the individual foundations. Each one went out with high hopes and each one came back — rejected.

Proposal after proposal was sent out and rejected. Finally, after the 155th grant proposal had been turned down, all of Rick's support began to crumble.

Rick's parents were begging him to go back to college and Ken Greene, an educator who had left his job to help Rick write proposals, said, "Rick, I have no money left and I have a wife and kids to support. I'll wait for one more proposal. But if it's a turndown, I'll have to go back to Toledo and to teaching."

Rick had one last chance. Activated by desperation and conviction, he managed to talk himself past several secretaries and he secured a lunch date with Dr. Russ Mawby, President of the Kellogg Foundation. On their way to lunch they passed an ice cream stand. "Would you like one?" Mawby asked. Rick nodded. But his anxiety got the better of him. He crushed the cone in his hand and, with chocolate ice cream running between his fingers, he made a surreptitious but frantic effort to shake it loose before Dr. Mawby could note what had happened. But Mawby did see it, and bursting into laughter, he went back to the vendor and brought Rick a bunch of paper napkins.

The young man climbed into the car, red-faced and miserable. How could he request funding for a new educational program when he couldn't even handle an ice cream cone?

Two weeks later Mawby phoned. "You asked for $55,000. We're sorry, but the trustees voted against it." Rick felt tears pressing behind his eyes. For two years he had been working for a dream, which would now go down the drain.

"However," said Mawby, "the trustees *did* vote unanimously to give you $130,000."

The tears came then. Rick could hardly even stammer out a thank you.

Since that time Rick Little has raised over $100,000,000 to fund his dream. The Quest Skills Programs are currently taught in over 30,000 schools in all 50 states and 32 countries. Three million kids per year are being taught important life skills because one 19-year-old refused to take "no" for an answer.

In 1989, because of the incredible success of Quest, Rick Little expanded his dream and was granted $65,000,000, the second largest grant ever given in U.S. history, to create The International Youth Foundation. The purpose of this foundation is to identify and expand successful youth programs all over the world.

Rick Little's life is a testament to the power of commitment to a high vision, coupled with a willingness to keep on asking until one manifests the dream.

Adapted from
Peggy Mann

The Magic Of Believing

I'm not old enough to play baseball or football. I'm not eight yet. My mom told me when you start baseball, you aren't going to be able to run that fast because you had an operation. I told Mom I wouldn't need to run that fast. When I play baseball, I'll just hit them out of the park. Then I'll be able to walk.

Edward J. McGrath, Jr.
"An Exceptional View of Life"

Glenna's Goal Book

In 1977 I was a single mother with three young daughters, a house payment, a car payment and a need to rekindle some dreams.

One evening I attended a seminar and heard a man speak on the I x V = R Principle. *(Imagination mixed with Vividness becomes Reality.)* The speaker pointed out that the mind thinks in pictures, not in words. And as we vividly picture in our mind what we desire, it will become a reality.

This concept struck a chord of creativity in my heart. I knew the Biblical truth that the Lord gives us "the desires of our heart" (Psalms 37:4) and that "as a man thinketh in his heart, so is he" (Proverbs 23:7). I was determined to take my written prayer list and turn it into pictures. I began cutting up old magazines and gathering pictures that depicted the "desires of my heart." I arranged them in an expensive photo album and waited expectantly.

I was very specific with my pictures. They included:

1. A good-looking man
2. A woman in a wedding gown and a man in a tuxedo
3. Bouquets of flowers (I'm a romantic)
4. Beautiful diamond jewelry (I rationalized that

God loved David and Solomon and they were two of the richest men who ever lived)
5. An island in the sparkling blue Caribbean
6. A lovely home
7. New furniture
8. A woman who had recently become vice-president of a large corporation. (I was working for a company that had no female officers. I wanted to be the first woman vice-president in that company.)

About eight weeks later, I was driving down a California freeway, minding my own business at 10:30 in the morning. Suddenly a gorgeous red-and-white Cadillac passed me. I looked at the car because it was a beautiful car. And the driver looked at me and smiled, and I smiled back because I always smile. Now I was in deep trouble. Have you ever done that? I tried to pretend that I hadn't looked. "Who me? I didn't look at you!" He followed me for the next 15 miles. Scared me to death! I drove a few miles, he drove a few miles. I parked, he parked . . . and eventually I married him!

On the first day after our first date, Jim sent me a dozen roses. Then I found out that he had a hobby. His hobby was collecting diamonds. Big ones! And he was looking for somebody to decorate. I volunteered! We dated for about two years and every Monday morning I received a long-stemmed red rose and a love note from him.

About three months before we were getting married, Jim said to me, "I have found the perfect place to go on our honeymoon. We will go to St. John's Island down in the Caribbean." I laughingly said, "I never would have thought of that!"

I did not confess the truth about my picture book until Jim and I had been married for almost a year. It was then that we were moving into our gorgeous new home and furnishing it with the elegant furniture that I had pictured. (Jim turned out to be the West Coast wholesale distributor for one of the finest eastern furniture manufacturers.)

By the way, the wedding was in Laguna Beach, California, and included the gown and tuxedo as realities. Eight months after I created my dream book, I became the Vice-President of Human Resources in the company where I worked.

In some sense this sounds like a fairy tale, but it is absolutely true. Jim and I have made many "picture books" since we have been married. God has filled our lives with the demonstration of these powerful principles of faith at work.

Decide what it is that you want in every area of your life. Imagine it vividly. Then act on your desires by actually constructing your personal goal book. Convert your ideas into concrete realities through this simple exercise. There are no impossible dreams. And, remember, God has promised to give His children the desires of their heart.

Glenna Salsbury

Another Check Mark On The List

One rainy afternoon an inspired 15-year-old boy named John Goddard sat down at his kitchen table in Los Angeles and wrote three words at the top of a yellow pad, "My Life List." Under that heading he wrote down 127 goals. Since then he has completed 108 of those goals. Look at the list of Goddard's goals which appears below. These are not simple or easy goals. They include climbing the world's major mountains, exploring vast waterways, running a mile in five minutes, reading the complete works of Shakespeare and reading the entire *Encyclopedia Britannica.*

Explore:

✓1. Nile River
✓2. Amazon River
✓3. Congo River
✓4. Colorado River
5. Yangtze River, China
6. Niger River
7. Orinoco River, Venezuela
✓8. Rio Coco, Nicaragua

Study Primitive Cultures In:

✓ 9. The Congo
✓10. New Guinea
✓11. Brazil
✓12. Borneo
✓13. The Sudan (John was nearly buried alive in a sandstorm.)
✓14. Australia
✓15. Kenya

✓16. The Philippines
✓17. Tanganyika (now Tanzania)
✓18. Ethiopia
✓19. Nigeria
✓20. Alaska

Climb:

21. Mount Everest
22. Mount Aconcagua, Argentina
23. Mount McKinley
✓24. Mount Huascaran, Peru
✓25. Mount Kilimanjaro
✓26. Mount Ararat, Turkey
✓27. Mount Kenya
28. Mount Cook, New Zealand
✓29. Mount Popocatepetl, Mexico
✓30. The Matterhorn
✓31. Mount Rainer
✓32. Mount Fuji
✓33. Mount Vesuvius
✓34. Mount Bromo, Java
✓35. Grand Tetons
✓36. Mount Baldy, California
✓37. Carry out careers in medicine and exploration (Studied pre-med and treats illnesses among primitive tribes)
38. Visit every country in the world (30 to go)
✓39. Study Navaho and Hopi Indians
✓40. Learn to fly a plane
✓41. Ride horse in Rose Parade

Photograph:

✓42. Iguacu Falls, Brazil
✓43. Victoria Falls, Rhodesia (Chased by a warthog in the process)
✓44. Sutherland Falls, New Zealand
✓45. Yosemite Falls
✓46. Niagara Falls
✓47. Retrace travels of Marco Polo and Alexander the Great

Explore Underwater:

✓48. Coral reefs of Florida
✓49. Great Barrier Reef, Australia (Photographed a 300-pound clam)
✓50. Red Sea
✓51. Fiji Islands
✓52. The Bahamas

✓53. Explore Okefenokee Swamp and the Everglades

Visit:

54. North and South Poles
✓55. Great Wall of China
✓56. Panama and Suez Canals
✓57. Easter Island
✓58. The Galapagos Islands
✓59. Vatican City (Saw the pope)
✓60. The Taj Mahal
✓61. The Eiffel Tower
✓62. The Blue Grotto
✓63. The Tower of London
✓64. The Leaning Tower of Pisa
✓65. The Sacred Well of Chichen-Itza, Mexico
✓66. Climb Ayers Rock in Australia
67. Follow River Jordan from Sea of Galilee to Dead Sea

Swim In:

✓ 68. Lake Victoria
✓69. Lake Superior
✓70. Lake Tanganyika
✓71. Lake Titicaca, South America
✓72. Lake Nicaragua

Accomplish:

✓ 73. Become an Eagle Scout
✓ 74. Dive in a submarine
✓75. Land on and take off from an aircraft carrier
✓ 76. Fly in a blimp, hot air balloon and glider
✓77. Ride an elephant, camel, ostrich and bronco
✓78. Skin dive to 40 feet and hold breath two and a half minutes underwater
✓79. Catch a ten-pound lobster and a ten-inch abalone
✓80. Play flute and violin
✓81. Type 50 words a minute
✓82. Take a parachute jump
✓83. Learn water and snow skiing

✓84. Go on a church mission
✓85. Follow the John Muir Trail
✓86. Study native medicines and bring back useful ones
✓87. Bag camera trophies of elephant, lion, rhino, cheetah, cape buffalo and whale
✓88. Learn to fence
✓89. Learn jujitsu
✓90. Teach a college course
✓91. Watch a cremation ceremony in Bali
✓92. Explore depths of the sea
93. Appear in a Tarzan movie (He now considers this an irrelevant boyhood dream)
94. Own a horse, chimpanzee, cheetah, ocelot and coyote (Yet to own a chimp or cheetah)
95. Become a ham radio operator
✓96. Build own telescope
✓97. Write a book (On Nile trip)
✓98. Publish an article in *National Geographic* Magazine
✓99. High jump five feet
✓100. Broad jump 15 feet
✓101. Run a mile in five minutes
✓102. Weigh 175 pounds stripped (still does)
✓103. Perform 200 sit-ups and 20 pull-ups
✓104. Learn French, Spanish and Arabic
105. Study dragon lizards on Komodo Island (Boat broke down within 20 miles of island)
✓106. Visit birthplace of Grandfather Sorenson in Denmark
✓107. Visit birthplace of Grandfather Goddard in England
✓108. Ship aboard a freighter as a seaman
109. Read the entire *Encyclopedia Britannica* (Has read extensive parts in each volume)
✓110. Read the Bible from cover to cover
✓111. Read the works of Shakespeare, Plato, Aristotle, Dickens, Thoreau, Poe,

Rousseau, Bacon, Hemingway, Twain, Burroughs, Conrad, Talmage, Tolstoi, Longfellow, Keats, Whittier and Emerson (Not every work of each)

✓112. Become familiar with the compositions of Bach, Beethoven, Debussy, Ibert, Mendelssohn, Lalo, Rimski-Korsakov, Respighi, Liszt, Rachmaninoff, Stravinsky, Toch, Tschaikovsky, Verdi

✓113. Become proficient in the use of a plane, motorcycle, tractor, surfboard, rifle, pistol, canoe, microscope, football, basket-ball, bow and arrow, lariat and boomerang

✓114. Compose music

✓115. Play *Clair de Lune* on the piano

✓116. Watch fire-walking ceremony (In Bali and Surinam)

✓117. Milk a poisonous snake (Bitten by a diamond back during a photo session)

✓118. Light a match with a 22 rifle

✓119. Visit a movie studio

✓120. Climb Cheops' pyramid

✓121. Become a member of the Explorers' Club and the Adventurers' Club

✓122. Learn to play polo

✓123. Travel through the Grand Canyon on foot and by boat

✓124. Circumnavigate the globe (four times)

125. Visit the moon ("Some-day if God wills")

✓126. Marry and have chil-dren (Has five children)

127. Live to see the 21st Century (He will be 75)

John Goddard

Willing To Pay The Price

When my wife Maryanne and I were building our Greenspoint Mall hair salon 13 years ago, a Vietnamese fellow would stop by each day to sell us doughnuts. He spoke hardly any English, but he was always friendly and through smiles and sign language, we got to know each other. His name was Le Van Vu.

During the day Le worked in a bakery and at night he and his wife listened to audio tapes to learn English. I later learned that they slept on sacks full of sawdust on the floor of the back room of the bakery.

In Vietnam the Van Vu family was one of the wealthiest in Southeast Asia. They owned almost one-third of North Vietnam, including huge holdings in industry and real estate. However, after his father was brutally murdered, Le moved to South Vietnam with his mother, where he went to school and eventually became a lawyer.

Like his father before him, Le prospered. He saw an opportunity to construct buildings to accommodate the ever-expanding American presence in South Vietnam and soon became one of the most successful builders in the country.

On a trip to the North, however, Le was captured by the North Vietnamese and thrown into prison for three years. He escaped by killing five soldiers and made his way back to South Vietnam where he was arrested again. The South Vietnamese government had assumed he was a "plant" from the North.

After serving time in prison, Le got out and started a fishing company, eventually becoming the largest canner in South Vietnam.

When Le learned that the U.S. troops and embassy personnel were about to pull out of his country, he made a life-changing decision.

He took all of the gold he had hoarded, loaded it aboard one of his fishing vessels and sailed with his wife out to the American ships in the harbor. He then exchanged all his riches for safe passage out of Vietnam to the Philippines, where he and his wife were taken into a refugee camp.

After gaining access to the president of the Philippines, Le convinced him to make one of his boats available for fishing and Le was back in business again. Before he left the Philippines two years later en route for America (his ultimate dream), Le had successfully developed the entire fishing industry in the Philippines.

But en route to America, Le became distraught and depressed about having to start over again with nothing. His wife tells of how she found him near the railing of the ship, about to jump overboard.

"Le," she told him, "if you do jump, whatever will become of me? We've been together for so long and through so much. We can do this together." It was all the encouragement that Le Van Vu needed.

When he and his wife arrived in Houston in 1972, they were flat broke and spoke no English. In Vietnam, family takes care of family, and Le and his wife found themselves ensconced in the back room of his cousin's bakery in the Greenspoint Mall. We were building our salon just a couple of hundred feet away.

Now, as they say, here comes the "message" part of this story:

Le's cousin offered both Le and his wife jobs in the bakery. After taxes, Le would take home $175 per week, his wife $125. Their total annual income, in other words, was $15,600. Further, his cousin offered to sell them the bakery whenever they could come up with a $30,000 down payment. The cousin would finance the remainder with a note for $90,000.

Here's what Le and his wife did:

Even with a weekly income of $300, they decided to continue to live in the back room. They kept clean by taking sponge baths for two years in the mall's restrooms. For two years their diet consisted almost entirely of bakery goods. Each year, for two years, they lived on a total, that's right, a total of $600, saving $30,000 for the down payment.

Le later explained his reasoning, "If we got ourselves an apartment, which we could afford on $300 per week, we'd have to pay the rent. Then, of course, we'd have to buy furniture. Then we'd have to have transportation to and from work, so that meant we'd have to buy a car. Then we'd have to buy gasoline for the car as well as insurance. Then we'd probably want to go places in the car, so that meant we'd need to buy clothes and toiletries. So I knew that if we got that apartment, we'd never get our $30,000 together."

Now, if you think you've heard everything about Le, let me tell you, there's more: After he and his wife had saved the $30,000 and bought the bakery, Le once again sat down with his wife for a serious chat. They still owed $90,000 to his cousin, he said, and as difficult as the past two years had been, they had to remain living in that back room for one more year.

I'm proud to tell you that in one year, my friend and mentor Le Van Vu and his wife, saving virtually every nickel of profit from the business, paid off the $90,000 note, and in just three years, owned an extremely profitable business free and clear.

Then, and only then, the Van Vus went out and got their first apartment. To this day, they continue to save on a regular basis, live on an extremely small percentage of their income, and, of course, always pay cash for any of their purchases.

Do you think that Le Van Vu is a millionaire today? I am happy to tell you, many times over.

John McCormack

Everybody Has A Dream

Some years ago I took on an assignment in a southern county to work with people on public welfare. What I wanted to do was show that everybody has the capacity to be self-sufficient and all we have to do is to activate them. I asked the county to pick a group of people who were on public welfare, people from different racial groups and different family constellations. I would then see them as a group for three hours every Friday. I also asked for a little petty cash to work with as I needed it.

The first thing I said after I shook hands with everybody was, "I would like to know what your dreams are." Everyone looked at me as if I were kind of wacky.

"Dreams? We don't have dreams."

I said, "Well, when you were a kid what happened? Wasn't there something you wanted to do?"

One woman said to me, "I don't know what you can do with dreams. The rats are eating up my kids."

"Oh," I said. "That's terrible. No, of course, you are very much involved with the rats and your kids. How can that be helped?"

"Well, I could use a new screen door because there are holes in my screen door."

I asked, "Is there anybody around here who knows how to fix a screen door?"

There was a man in the group, and he said, "A long time ago I used to do things like that but now I have a terribly bad back, but I'll try."

I told him I had some money if he would go to the store and buy some screening and go and fix the lady's screen door. "Do you think you can do that?"

"Yes, I'll try."

The next week, when the group was seated, I said to the woman, "Well, is your screen door fixed?"

"Oh, yes," she said.

"Then we can start dreaming, can't we?" She sort of smiled at me.

I said to the man who did the work, "How do you feel?"

He said, "Well, you know, it's a very funny thing. I'm beginning to feel a lot better."

That helped the group to begin to dream. These seemingly small successes allowed the group to see that dreams were not insane. These small steps began to get people to see and feel that something really could happen.

I began to ask other people about their dreams. One woman shared that she always wanted to be a secretary. I said, "Well, what stands in your way?" (That's always my next question.)

She said, "I have six kids, and I don't have anyone to take care of them while I'm away."

"Let's find out," I said. "Is there anybody in this group who would take care of six kids for a day or two a week while this woman gets some training here at the community college?"

One woman said "I got kids, too, but I could do that."

"Let's do it," I said. So a plan was created and the woman went to school.

Everyone found something. The man who put in the screen door became a handyman. The woman who took in the children became a licensed foster care person. In 12 weeks I had all these people off public welfare. I've not only done that once, I've done it many times.

Virginia Satir

Follow Your Dream

I have a friend named Monty Roberts who owns a horse ranch in San Ysidro. He has let me use his house to put on fund-raising events to raise money for youth at risk programs.

The last time I was there he introduced me by saying, "I want to tell you why I let Jack use my house. It all goes back to a story about a young man who was the son of an itinerant horse trainer who would go from stable to stable, race track to race track, farm to farm and ranch to ranch, training horses. As a result, the boy's high school career was continually interrupted. When he was a senior, he was asked to write a paper about what he wanted to be and do when he grew up.

"That night he wrote a seven-page paper describing his goal of someday owning a horse ranch. He wrote about his dream in great detail and he even drew a diagram of a 200-acre ranch, showing the location of all the buildings, the stables and the track. Then he drew a detailed floor plan for a 4,000-square-foot house that would sit on the 200-acre dream ranch.

"He put a great deal of his heart into the project and the next day he handed it in to his teacher. Two days later he received his paper back. On the front page was a large red F with a note that read, 'See me after class.'

"The boy with the dream went to see the teacher after class and asked, 'Why did I receive an F?'

"The teacher said, 'This is an unrealistic dream for a young boy like you. You have no money. You come from an itinerant family. You have no resources. Owning a horse ranch requires a lot of money. You have to buy the land. You have to pay for the original breeding stock and later you'll have to pay large stud fees. There's no way you could ever do it.' Then the teacher added, 'If you will rewrite this paper with a more realistic goal, I will reconsider your grade.'

"The boy went home and thought about it long and hard. He asked his father what he should do. His father said, 'Look, son, you have to make up your own mind on this. However, I think it is a very important decision for you.'

"Finally, after sitting with it for a week, the boy turned in the same paper, making no changes at all. He stated, 'You can keep the F and I'll keep my dream.' "

Monty then turned to the assembled group and said, "I tell you this story because you are sitting in my 4,000-square-foot house in the middle of my 200-acre horse ranch. I still have that school paper framed over the fireplace." He added, "The best part of the story is that two summers ago that same schoolteacher brought 30 kids to camp out on my ranch for a week." When the teacher was leaving, he said, 'Look, Monty, I can tell you this now. When I was your teacher, I was something of a dream stealer. During those years I stole a lot of kids' dreams. Fortunately you had enough gumption not to give up on yours.' "

Don't let anyone steal your dreams. Follow your heart, no matter what.

Jack Canfield

The Box

When I was a senior in college, I came home for Christmas vacation and anticipated a fun-filled fortnight with my two brothers. We were so excited to be together, we volunteered to watch the store so that my mother and father could take their first day off in years. The day before my parents went to Boston, my father took me quietly aside to the little den behind the store. The room was so small that it held only a piano and a hide-a-bed couch. In fact, when you pulled the bed out, it filled the room and you could sit on the foot of it and play the piano. Father reached behind the old upright and pulled out a cigar box. He opened it and showed me a little pile of newspaper articles. I had read so many Nancy Drew detective stories that I was excited and wide-eyed over the hidden box of clippings.

"What are they?" I asked.

Father replied seriously, "These are articles I've written and some letters to the editor that have been published."

As I began to read, I saw at the bottom of each neatly clipped article the name Walter Chapman, Esq. "Why didn't you tell me you'd done this?" I asked.

"Because I didn't want your mother to know. She has always told me that since I didn't have much education, I shouldn't try to write. I wanted to run for some political office also, but she told me I shouldn't try. I guess she was afraid she'd be embarrassed if I lost. I just wanted to try for the fun of it. I figured I could write without her knowing it, and so I did. When each item would be printed, I'd cut it out and hide it in this box. I knew someday I'd show the box to someone, and it's you."

He watched me as I read over a few of the articles and when I looked up, his big blue eyes were moist. "I guess I tried for something too big this last time," he added.

"Did you write something else?"

"Yes, I sent some suggestions in to our denominational magazine on how the national nominating committee could be selected more fairly. It's been three months since I sent it in. I guess I tried for something too big."

This was such a new side to my fun-loving father that I didn't quite know what to say, so I tried, "Maybe it'll still come."

"Maybe, but don't hold your breath." Father gave me a little smile and a wink and then closed the cigar box and tucked it into the space behind the piano.

The next morning our parents left on the bus to the Haverhill Depot where they took a train to Boston. Jim, Ron and I ran the store and I thought about the box. I'd never known my father liked to write. I didn't tell my brothers; it was a secret between Father and me. The Mystery of the Hidden Box.

Early that evening I looked out the store window and saw my mother get off the bus — alone. She crossed the Square and walked briskly through the store.

"Where's Dad?" we asked together.

"Your father's dead," she said without a tear.

In disbelief we followed her to the kitchen where she told us they had been walking through the Park Street Subway Station in the midst of crowds of people when Father had fallen to the floor. A nurse bent over him, looked up at Mother and said simply, "He's dead."

Mother had stood by him stunned, not knowing what to do as people tripped over him in their rush through the subway. A priest said, "I'll call the police," and disappeared. Mother straddled Dad's body for about an hour. Finally an ambulance came and took them both to the only morgue where Mother had to go through his pockets and remove his watch. She'd come back on the train alone and then home on the local bus. Mother told us the shocking tale without shedding a tear. Not showing emotion had always been a matter of discipline and pride for her. We didn't cry either and we took turns waiting on the customers.

One steady patron asked, "Where's the old man tonight?"

"He's dead," I replied.

"Oh, too bad," and he left.

I'd not thought of him as the old man, and I was mad at the question, but he was 70 and Mother was only 50. He'd always been healthy and happy and he'd cared for frail mother without complaining and now he was gone. No more whistling, no more singing hymns while stocking shelves. The "old man" was gone.

On the morning of the funeral, I sat at the table in the store opening sympathy cards and pasting them in a scrapbook when I noticed the church magazine in the pile. Normally I would never have opened what I viewed as a dull religious publication, but just maybe that sacred article might be there — and it was.

I took the magazine to the little den, shut the door, and burst into tears. I'd been brave, but seeing Dad's bold recommendations to the national convention in print was more than I could bear. I read and cried and then I read again. I pulled out the box from behind the piano and under the clippings I found a two-page letter to my father from Henry Cabot Lodge, Sr., thanking him for his campaign suggestions.

I didn't tell anyone about my box. It remained a secret.

Florence Littauer

Encouragement

Some of the greatest success stories of history have followed a word of encouragement or an act of confidence by a loved one or a trusting friend. Had it not been for a confident wife, Sophia, we might not have listed among the great names of literature the name of Nathaniel Hawthorne. When Nathaniel, a heartbroken man, went home to tell his wife that he was a failure and had been fired from his job in a customhouse, she surprised him with an exclamation of joy.

"Now," she said triumphantly, "you can write your book!"

"Yes," replied the man, with sagging confidence, "and what shall we live on while I am writing it?"

To his amazement, she opened a drawer and pulled out a substantial amount of money.

"Where on earth did you get that?" he exclaimed.

"I have always known you were a man of genius," she told him. "I knew that someday you would write a masterpiece. So every week, out of the money you gave me for housekeeping, I saved a little bit. So here is enough to last us for one whole year."

From her trust and confidence came one of the greatest novels of American literature, *The Scarlet Letter.*

Nido Qubein

Are You Strong Enough To Handle Critics?

It is not the critic who counts, not the man who points out how the strong man stumbles or where the doer of deeds could have done them better. The credit belongs to the man who is actually in the arena, whose face is marred by dust and sweat and blood, who strives valiantly, who errs and comes short again and again because there is no effort without error and shortcomings, who knows the great devotion, who spends himself in a worthy cause, who at best knows in the end the high achievement of triumph and who at worst, if he fails while daring greatly, knows his place shall never be with those timid and cold souls who know neither victory nor defeat.

Theodore Roosevelt

Risking

Two seeds lay side by side in the fertile spring soil.

The first seed said, "I want to grow! I want to send my roots deep into the soil beneath me, and thrust my sprouts through the earth's crust above me . . . I want to unfurl my tender buds like banners to announce the arrival of spring . . . I want to feel the warmth of the sun on my face and the blessing of the morning dew on my petals!"

And so she grew.

The second seed said, "I am afraid. If I send my roots into the ground below, I don't know what I will encounter in the dark. If I push my way through the hard soil above me I may damage my delicate sprouts . . . what if I let my buds open and a snail tries to eat them? And if I were to open my blossoms, a small child may pull me from the ground. No, it is much better for me to wait until it is safe."

And so she waited.

A yard hen scratching around in the early spring ground for food found the waiting seed and promptly ate it.

MORAL OF THE STORY

Those of us who refuse to risk and grow
get swallowed up by life.

Patty Hansen

Try Something Different

When we first read the following story, we had just begun teaching a course called "The Million Dollar Forum," a course designed to teach people to accelerate their income up to levels of a million dollars a year or more. Early on we discovered people get locked into a rut of trying harder without trying smarter. Trying harder doesn't always work. Sometimes we need to do something radically different to achieve greater levels of success. We need to break out of our paradigm prisons, our habit patterns and our comfort zones.

•••

I'm sitting in a quiet room at the Milcroft Inn, a peaceful little place hidden back among the pine trees about an hour out of Toronto. It's just past noon, late July, and I'm listening to the desperate sounds of a life-or-death struggle going on a few feet away.

There's a small fly burning out the last of its short life's energies in a futile attempt to fly through the glass of the windowpane. The whining wings tell the poignant story of the fly's strategy: *Try harder.*

But it's not working.

The frenzied effort offers no hope for survival. Ironically, the struggle is part of the trap. It is impossible for the fly to try hard enough to succeed at breaking through the glass. Nevertheless, this little insect has staked its life on reaching its goal through raw effort and determination.

This fly is doomed. It will die there on the windowsill.

Across the room, ten steps away, the door is open. Ten seconds of flying time and this small creature could reach the outside world it seeks. With only a fraction of the effort now being wasted, it could be free of this self-imposed trap. The breakthrough possibility is there. It would be so easy.

Why doesn't the fly try another approach, something dramatically different? How did it get so locked in on the idea that this particular route and determined effort offer the most promise for success? What logic is there in continuing until death to seek a breakthrough with more of the same?

No doubt this approach makes sense to the fly. Regrettably, it's an idea that will kill.

Trying harder isn't necessarily the solution to achieving more. It may not offer any real promise for getting what you want out of life. Sometimes, in fact, it's a big part of the problem.

If you stake your hopes for a breakthrough on trying harder than ever, you may kill your chances for success.

Price Pritchett

Service With A Smile

A man wrote a letter to a small hotel in a midwest town he planned to visit on his vacation. He wrote:

> I would very much like to bring my dog with me. He is well-groomed and very well behaved. Would you be willing to permit me to keep him in my room with me at night?

An immediate reply came from the hotel owner, who said,

> I've been operating this hotel for many years. In all that time, I've never had a dog steal towels, bed clothes or silverware or pictures off the walls.
>
> I've never had to evict a dog in the middle of the night for being drunk and disorderly. And I've never had a dog run out on a hotel bill.
>
> Yes, indeed, your dog is welcome at my hotel. And, if your dog will vouch for you, you're welcome to stay here, too.

Karl Albrecht and *Ron Zenke*
Service America

6

OVERCOMING OBSTACLES

Obstacles are those frightful things you see when you take your eyes off your goal.

Henry Ford

Obstacles

We who lived in the concentration camps can remember the men who walked through the huts comforting others, giving away their last piece of bread. They may have been few in number, but they offer sufficient proof that everything can be taken from a man but one thing: The last of his freedoms — to choose one's attitude in any given set of circumstances, to choose one's own way.

Viktor E. Frankl
Man's Search for Meaning

Consider This

Consider this:

- After Fred Astaire's first screen test, the memo from the testing director of MGM, dated 1933, said, "Can't act! Slightly bald! Can dance a little!" Astaire kept that memo over the fireplace in his Beverly Hills home.
- An expert said of Vince Lombardi: "He possesses minimal football knowledge. Lacks motivation."
- Socrates was called, "An immoral corrupter of youth."
- When Peter J. Daniel was in the fourth grade, his teacher, Mrs. Phillips, constantly said, "Peter J. Daniel, you're no good, you're a bad apple and you're never going to amount to anything." Peter was totally illiterate until he was 26. A friend stayed up with him all night and read him a copy of *Think and Grow Rich.* Now he owns the street corners he used to fight on and just published his latest book: *Mrs. Phillips, You Were Wrong!*
- Louisa May Alcott, the author of *Little Women,* was encouraged to find work as a servant or seamstress by her family.
- Beethoven handled the violin awkwardly and preferred playing his own compositions instead of

improving his technique. His teacher called him hopeless as a composer.

- The parents of the famous opera singer Enrico Caruso wanted him to be an engineer. His teacher said he had no voice at all and could not sing.
- Charles Darwin, father of the Theory of Evolution, gave up a medical career and was told by his father, "You care for nothing but shooting, dogs and rat catching." In his autobiography, Darwin wrote, "I was considered by all my masters and by my father, a very ordinary boy, rather below the common standard in intellect."
- Walt Disney was fired by a newspaper editor for lack of ideas. Walt Disney also went bankrupt several times before he built Disneyland.
- Thomas Edison's teachers said he was too stupid to learn anything.
- Albert Einstein did not speak until he was four years old and didn't read until he was seven. His teacher described him as "mentally slow, unsociable and adrift forever in his foolish dreams." He was expelled and was refused admittance to the Zurich Polytechnic School.
- Louis Pasteur was only a mediocre pupil in undergraduate studies and ranked 15th out of 22 in chemistry.
- Isaac Newton did very poorly in grade school.
- The sculptor Rodin's father said, "I have an idiot for a son." Described as the worst pupil in the school, Rodin failed three times to secure admittance to the school of art. His uncle called him uneducable.
- Leo Tolstoy, author of *War and Peace,* flunked out of college. He was described as "both unable and unwilling to learn."

- Playwright Tennessee Williams was enraged when his play *Me, Vasha* was not chosen in a class competition at Washington University where he was enrolled in English XVI. The teacher recalled that Williams denounced the judges' choices and their intelligence.
- F.W. Woolworth's employers at the dry goods store said he had not enough sense to wait upon customers.
- Henry Ford failed and went broke five times before he finally succeeded.
- Babe Ruth, considered by sports historians to be the greatest athlete of all time and famous for setting the home run record, also holds the record for strikeouts.
- Winston Churchill failed sixth grade. He did not become Prime Minister of England until he was 62, and then only after a lifetime of defeats and setbacks. His greatest contributions came when he was a "senior citizen."
- Eighteen publishers turned down Richard Bach's 10,000-word story about a "soaring" seagull, *Jonathan Livingston Seagull,* before Macmillan finally published it in 1970. By 1975 it had sold more than seven million copies in the U.S. alone.
- Richard Hooker worked for seven years on his humorous war novel, *M*A*S*H,* only to have it rejected by 21 publishers before Morrow decided to publish it. It became a runaway bestseller, spawning a blockbusting movie and a highly successful television series.

Jack Canfield and Mark V. Hansen

John Corcoran — The Man Who Couldn't Read

For as long as John Corcoran could remember, words had mocked him. The letters in sentences traded places, vowel sounds lost themselves in the tunnels of his ears. In school he'd sit at his desk, stupid and silent as a stone, knowing he would be different from everyone else forever. If only someone had sat next to that little boy, put an arm around his shoulder and said, "I'll help you. Don't be scared."

But no one had heard of dyslexia then. And John couldn't tell them that the left side of his brain, the lobe humans use to arrange symbols logically in a sequence, had always misfired.

Instead, in second grade they put him in the "dumb" row. In third grade a nun handed a yardstick to the other children when John refused to read or write and let each student have a crack at his legs. In fourth grade his teacher called on him to read and let one minute of quiet pile upon another until the child thought he would suffocate. Then he was passed on to the next grade and the next. John Corcoran never failed a year in his life.

In his senior year, John was voted homecoming king, went steady with the valedictorian and starred on the basketball team. His mom kissed him when he graduated — and kept talking about college. College? It would be insane to consider. But he finally decided on the University of Texas at El Paso where he could try out for the basketball team. He took a deep breath, closed his eyes . . . and recrossed enemy lines.

On campus John asked each new friend: Which teachers gave essay tests? Which gave multiple choice? The minute he stepped out of a class, he tore the pages of scribble from his notebook, in case anyone asked to see his notes. He stared at thick textbooks in the evening so his roommate wouldn't doubt. And he lay in bed, exhausted but unable to sleep, unable to make his whirring mind let go. John promised he'd go to Mass 30 days straight at the crack of dawn, if only God would let him get his degree.

He got the diploma. He gave God his 30 days of Mass. Now what? Maybe he was addicted to the edge. Maybe the thing he felt most insecure about — his mind — was what he needed most to have admired. Maybe that's why, in 1961, John became a teacher.

John taught in California. Each day he had a student read the textbook to the class. He gave standardized tests that he could grade by placing a form with holes over each correct answer and he lay in bed for hours on weekend mornings, depressed.

Then he met Kathy, an A student and a nurse. Not a leaf, like John. A rock. "There's something I have to tell you, Kathy," he said one night in 1965 before their marriage, "I . . . I can't read."

"He's a teacher," she thought. He must mean he can't read well. Kathy didn't understand until years later when she saw John unable to read a children's book to their 18-month-old daughter. Kathy filled out his forms, read and wrote his letters. Why didn't he simply ask her to teach him to read and write? He couldn't believe that anyone could teach him.

At age 28 John borrowed $2,500, bought a second house, fixed it up and rented it. He bought and rented another. And another. His business got bigger and bigger until he needed a secretary, a lawyer and a partner.

Then one day his accountant told him he was a millionaire. Perfect. Who'd notice that a millionaire always pulled on the doors that said PUSH or paused before entering public bathrooms, waiting to see which one the men walked out of?

In 1982 the bottom began to fall out. His properties started to sit empty and investors pulled out. Threats of foreclosures and lawsuits tumbled out of envelopes. Every waking moment, it seemed, he was pleading with bankers to extend his loans, coaxing builders to stay on the job, trying to make sense of the pyramid of paper. Soon he knew they'd have him on the witness stand and the man in black robes would say: "The truth, John Corcoran. Can't you even read?"

Finally in the fall of 1986, at age 48, John did two things he swore he never would. He put up his house as collateral to obtain one last construction loan. And he walked into the Carlsbad City Library and told the woman in charge of the tutoring program, "I can't read."

Then he cried.

He was placed with a 65-year-old grandmother named Eleanor Condit. Painstakingly — letter by letter, phonetically — she began teaching him. Within 14 months, his land-development company began to revive. And John Corcoran was learning to read.

The next step was confession: a speech before 200 stunned businessmen in San Diego. To heal, he had to come clean. He was placed on the board of directors of the San Diego Council on Literacy and began traveling across the country to give speeches.

"Illiteracy is a form of slavery!" he would cry. "We can't waste time blaming anyone. We need to become obsessed with teaching people to read!"

He read every book or magazine he could get his hands on, every road sign he passed, out loud, as long as Kathy could bear it. It was glorious, like singing And now he could sleep.

Then one day it occurred to him — one more thing he could finally do. Yes, that dusty box in his office, that sheaf of papers bound by ribbon . . . a quarter-century later, John Corcoran could read his wife's love letters.

Gary Smith

Don't Be Afraid To Fail

You've failed many times, although you may not remember.
You fell down the first time you tried to walk.
You almost drowned the first time you tried to swim, didn't you?
Did you hit the ball the first time you swung a bat?
Heavy hitters, the ones who hit the most home runs, also strike out a lot.
R.H. Macy failed seven times before his store in New York caught on.
English novelist John Creasey got 753 rejection slips before he published 564 books.
Babe Ruth struck out 1,330 times, but he also hit 714 home runs.
Don't worry about failure.
Worry about the chances you miss when you don't *even try.*

A message as published in the *Wall Street Journal* by United Technologies Corporation, Hartford, Connecticut 06101

Abraham Lincoln Didn't Quit

The sense of obligation to continue is present in all of us. A duty to strive is the duty of us all. I felt a call to that duty.

Abraham Lincoln

Probably the greatest example of persistence is Abraham Lincoln. If you want to learn about somebody who didn't quit, look no further.

Born into poverty, Lincoln was faced with defeat throughout his life. He lost eight elections, twice failed in business and suffered a nervous breakdown.

He could have quit many times — but he didn't and because he didn't quit, he became one of the greatest presidents in the history of our country.

Lincoln was a champion and he never gave up. Here is a sketch of Lincoln's road to the White House:

1816 His family was forced out of their home. He had to work to support them.

1818 His mother died.

1831 Failed in business.

1832 Ran for state legislature — *lost.*

1832 Also lost his job — wanted to go to law school but couldn't get in.

1833 Borrowed some money from a friend to begin a business and by the end of the year he was bankrupt. He spent the next 17 years of his life paying off this debt.

1834 Ran for state legislature again — *won.*

1835 Was engaged to be married, sweetheart died and his heart was broken.

1836 Had a total nervous breakdown and was in bed for six months.

1838 Sought to become speaker of the state legislature — *defeated.*

1840 Sought to become elector — *defeated.*

1843 Ran for Congress — *lost.*

1846 Ran for Congress again — *this time he won* — went to Washington and did a good job.

1848 Ran for re-election to Congress — *lost.*

1849 Sought the job of land officer in his home state — *rejected.*

1854 Ran for Senate of the United States — *lost.*

1856 Sought the Vice-Presidential nomination at his party's national convention — got less than 100 votes.

1858 Ran for U.S. Senate again — *again he lost.*

1860 *Elected president of the United States.*

The path was worn and slippery. My foot slipped from under me, knocking the other out of the way, but I recovered and said to myself, "It's a slip and not a fall."

Abraham Lincoln
After losing a senate race

Lesson From A Son

My son Daniel's passion for surfing began at the age of 13. Before and after school each day, he donned his wet suit, paddled out beyond the surf line and waited to be challenged by his three- to six-foot companions. Daniel's love of the ride was tested one fateful afternoon.

"Your son's been in an accident," the lifeguard reported over the phone to my husband Mike.

"How bad?"

"Bad. When he surfaced to the top of the water, the point of the board was headed toward his eye."

Mike rushed him to the emergency room and they were then sent to a plastic surgeon's office. He received 26 stitches from the corner of his eye to the bridge of his nose.

I was on an airplane flying home from a speaking engagement while Dan's eye was being stitched. Mike drove directly to the airport after they left the doctor's office. He greeted me at the gate and told me Dan was waiting in the car.

"Daniel?" I questioned. I remember thinking the waves must have been lousy that day.

"He's been in an accident, but he's going to be fine."

A traveling working mother's worst nightmare had come true. I ran to the car so fast the heel of my shoe broke off. I swung open the door, and my youngest son with the patched eye was leaning forward with both arms stretched out toward me crying, "Oh, Ma, I'm so glad you're home."

I sobbed in his arms telling him how awful I felt about not being there when the lifeguard called.

"It's okay, Mom," he comforted me. "You don't know how to surf anyway."

"What?" I asked, confused by his logic.

"I'll be fine. The doctor says I can go back in the water in eight days."

Was he out of his mind? I wanted to tell him he wasn't allowed to go near water again until he was 35, but instead I bit my tongue and prayed he would forget about surfing forevermore.

For the next seven days he kept pressing me to let him go back on the board. One day after I emphatically repeated "No" to him for the 100th time, he beat me at my own game.

"Mom, you taught us never to give up what we love."

Then he handed me a bribe -- a framed poem by Langston Hughes that he bought "because it reminded me of you."

Mother To Son

Well, son, I'll tell you:
Life for me ain't been no crystal stair.
It's had tacks in it.
And splinters,
And boards torn up,
And places with no carpet on the floor —
Bare.
But all the time
I'se been a-climbin' on,

And reachin' landin's
And turnin' corners,
And sometimes goin' in the dark
Where there ain't been no light.
So, boy, don't you turn back,
Don't you set down on the steps
'Cause you finds it's kinder hard.
Don't you fall now —
For I'se still goin', honey,
I'se still climbin'
And life for me ain't been no crystal stair.

I gave in.

Back then Daniel was a just a boy with a passion for surfing. Now he's a man with a responsibility. He ranks among the top 25 pro surfers in the world.

I was tested in my own backyard on an important principle that I teach audiences in distant cities: "Passionate people embrace what they love and never give up."

Danielle Kennedy

. . . AND EVER SINCE I FOUND OUT THAT BABE RUTH STRUCK OUT 1,330 TIMES . . . . I'VE BEEN FEELING LOTS BETTER !!

Failure? No! Just Temporary Setbacks

To see things in the seed, that is genius.

Lao-tzu

If you could come to my office in California to visit with me today, you would notice across one side of the room a beautiful old-fashioned Spanish tile and mahogany soda fountain with nine leather-covered stools (the kind they used to have in the old drug stores). Unusual? Yes. But if those stools could speak, they would tell you a story about the day I almost lost hope and gave up.

It was a recession period after World War II and jobs were scarce. Cowboy Bob, my husband, had purchased a small dry cleaning business with borrowed money. We had two darling babies, a tract home, a car and all the usual time payments. Then the bottom fell out. There was no money for the house payments or anything else.

I felt that I had no special talent, no training, no college education. I didn't think much of myself. But I remembered someone in my past who thought I had a little ability — my Alhambra High School English teacher. She inspired me to take journalism and named me advertising manager and feature editor of the school paper. I thought, "Now if I could write a 'Shoppers Column' for the small weekly newspaper in our rural town, maybe I could earn that house payment."

I had no car and no baby-sitter. So I pushed my two children before me in a rickety baby stroller with a big pillow tied in the back. The wheel kept coming off, but I hit it back on with the heel of my shoe and kept going. I was determined that my children would not lose their home as I often had done as a child.

But at the newspaper office, there were no jobs available. Recession. So I caught an idea. I asked if I might buy advertising space at wholesale and sell it at retail as a "Shoppers Column." They agreed, telling me later that they mentally gave me about a week of pushing that beat-up heavily laden stroller down those country roads before I gave up. But they were wrong.

The newspaper column idea worked. I made enough money for the house payment and to buy an old used car that Cowboy Bob found for me. Then I hired a high school girl to baby-sit from three to five each afternoon. When the clock struck three, I grabbed my newspaper samples and flew out of the door to drive to my appointments.

But on one dark rainy afternoon every advertising prospect I had worked on turned me down when I went to pick up their copy.

"Why?" I asked. They said they had noticed that Ruben Ahlman, the President of the Chamber of Commerce and the owner of the Rexall Drug store did not advertise with me. His store was the most popular in town. They respected his judgment. "There must be something wrong with your advertising," they explained.

My heart sank. Those four ads would have made the house payment. Then I thought, I will try to speak with Mr. Ahlman one more time. Everyone loves and respects him. Surely he will listen. Every time I had tried to approach him in the past, he had refused to see me. He was always "out" or unavailable. I knew that if he advertised with me, the other merchants in town would follow his lead.

This time, as I walked into the Rexall drug store, he was there at the prescription counter in the back. I smiled my best smile and held up my precious "Shoppers Column" carefully marked in my children's green crayola. I said, "Everyone respects your opinion, Mr. Ahlman. Would you just look at my work for a moment so that I can tell the other merchants what you think?"

His mouth turned perpendicular in an upside down U. Without saying a word he emphatically shook his head in the chilling negative gesture, "NO!" My knotted heart fell to the floor with such a thud, I thought everyone must have heard it.

Suddenly all of my enthusiasm left me. I made it as far as the beautiful old soda fountain at the front of the drug store, feeling that I didn't have the strength to drive home. I didn't want to sit at the soda fountain without buying something, so I pulled out my last dime and ordered a cherry Coke. I wondered desperately what to do. Would my babies lose their home as I had so many times when I was growing up? Was my journalism teacher wrong? Maybe that talent she talked about was just a dud. My eyes filled with tears.

A soft voice beside me on the next soda fountain stool said, "What is the matter, dear?" I looked up into the sympathetic face of a lovely grey haired lady. I poured out my story to her, ending it with, "But Mr. Ahlman, who everyone respects so much, will not look at my work."

"Let me see that Shoppers Column," she said. She took my marked issue of the newspaper in her hands and carefully read it all the way through. Then she spun around on the stool, stood up, looked back at the prescription counter and in a commanding voice that could be heard down the block, said, "Ruben Ahlman, come *here!*" The lady was Mrs. Ahlman!

She told Ruben to buy the advertising from me. His mouth turned up the other way in a big grin. Then she asked me for the names of the four merchants who had turned me down. She went to the phone and called each one. She gave me a hug and told me they were waiting for me and to go back and pick up their ads.

Ruben and Vivian Ahlman became our dear friends, as well as steady advertising customers. I learned that Ruben was a darling man who bought from everyone. He had promised Vivian not to buy any more advertising. He was just trying to keep his word to her. If I had only asked others in town, I might have learned that I should have been talking to Mrs. Ahlman from the beginning. That conversation on the stools of the soda fountain was the turning point. My advertising business prospered and grew into four offices, with 285 employees serving 4,000 continuous contract advertising accounts.

Later when Mr. Ahlman modernized the old drug store and removed the soda fountain, my sweet husband Bob bought it and installed it in my office. If you were here in California, we would sit on the soda fountain stools together. I'd pour you a cherry Coke and remind you to never give up, to remember that help is always closer than we know.

Then I would tell you that if you can't communicate with a key person, search for more information. Try another path around. Look for someone who can communicate for you in a third person endorsement. And, finally, I would serve you these sparkling, refreshing words of Bill Marriott of the Marriott Hotels:

> *Failure? I never encountered it.*
> *All I ever met were temporary setbacks.*

Dottie Walters

For Me To Be More Creative, I Am Waiting For . . .

1. Inspiration
2. Permission
3. Reassurance
4. The coffee to be ready
5. My turn
6. Someone to smooth the way
7. The rest of the rules
8. Someone to change
9. Wider fairways
10. Revenge
11. The stakes to be lower
12. More time
13. A significant relationship to:
    (a) improve
    (b) terminate
    (c) happen
14. The right person
15. A disaster
16. Time to almost run out
17. An obvious scapegoat
18. The kids to leave home
19. A Dow-Jones of 1500
20. The Lion to lie down with the Lamb
21. Mutual consent
22. A better time
23. A more favorable horoscope
24. My youth to return
25. The two-minute warning
26. The legal profession to reform
27. Richard Nixon to be re-elected
28. Age to grant me the right of eccentricity
29. Tomorrow
30. Jacks or better
31. My annual checkup
32. A better circle of friends
33. The stakes to be higher
34. The semester to start
35. My way to be clear
36. The cat to stop clawing the sofa
37. An absence of risk

38. The barking dog next door to leave town
39. My uncle to come home from the service
40. Someone to discover me
41. More adequate safeguards
42. A lower capital gains rate
43. The statute of limitations to run out
44. My parents to die (Joke!)
45. A cure for herpes/AIDS
46. The things that I do not understand or approve of to go away
47. Wars to end
48. My love to rekindle
49. Someone to be watching
50. A clearly written set of instructions
51. Better birth control
52. The ERA to pass
53. An end to poverty, injustice, cruelty, deceit, incompetence, pestilence, crime and offensive suggestions
54. A competing patent to expire
55. Chicken Little to return
56. My subordinates to mature
57. My ego to improve
58. The pot to boil
59. My new credit card
60. The piano tuner
61. This meeting to be over
62. My receivables to clear
63. The unemployment checks to run out
64. Spring
65. My suit to come back from the cleaners
66. My self-esteem to be restored
67. A signal from Heaven
68. The alimony payments to stop
69. The gems of brilliance buried within my first bumbling efforts to be recognized, applauded and substantially rewarded so that I can work on the second draft in comfort
70. A reinterpretation of *Robert's Rules of Order*
71. Various aches and pains to subside
72. Shorter lines at the bank
73. The wind to freshen
74. My children to be thoughtful, neat, obedient and self-supporting
75. Next season
76. Someone else to screw up
77. My current life to be declared a dress rehearsal with some script changes permitted before opening night
78. Logic to prevail
79. The next time around
80. You to stand out of my light

81. My ship to come in
82. A better deodorant
83. My dissertation to be finished
84. A sharp pencil
85. The check to clear
86. My wife, film or boomerang to come back
87. My doctor's approval, my father's permission, my minister's blessing or my lawyer's okay
88. Morning
89. California to fall into the ocean
90. A less turbulent time
91. The Iceman to Cometh
92. An opportunity to call collect
93. A better write-off
94. My smoking urges to subside
95. The rates to go down
96. The rates to go up
97. The rates to stabilize
98. My grandfather's estate to be settled
99. Weekend rates
100. A cue card
101. You to go first

David B. Campbell

Everybody Can Do Something

The basic difference between an ordinary man and a warrior is that a warrior takes everything as a challenge, while an ordinary man takes everything either as a blessing or a curse.

Don Juan

Roger Crawford had everything he needed to play tennis — except two hands and a leg.

When Roger's parents saw their son for the first time, they saw a baby with a thumb-like projection extended directly out of his right forearm and a thumb and one finger stuck out of his left forearm. He had no palms. The baby's arms and legs were shortened, and he had only three toes on his shrunken right foot and a withered left leg, which would later be amputated.

The doctor said Roger suffered from ectrodactylism, a rare birth defect affecting only one out of 90,000 children born in the United States. The doctor said Roger would probably never walk or care for himself.

Fortunately Roger's parents didn't believe the doctor.

"My parents always taught me that I was only as handicapped as I wanted to be," said Roger. "They never allowed me to feel sorry for myself or take advantage of people because of my handicap. Once I got into trouble because my school papers were continually late," explained Roger, who had to hold his pencil with both "hands" to write slowly. "I asked Dad to write a note to my teachers, asking for a two-day extension on my assignments. Instead Dad made me start writing my paper two days early!"

Roger's father always encouraged him to get involved in sports, teaching Roger to catch and throw a volleyball, and play backyard football after school. At age 12, Roger managed to win a spot on the school football team.

Before every game, Roger would visualize his dream of scoring a touchdown. Then one day he got his chance. The ball landed in his arms and off he ran as fast as he could on his artificial leg toward the goal line, his coach and teammates cheering wildly. But at the ten-yard line, a guy from the other team caught up with Roger, grabbing his left ankle. Roger tried to pull his artificial leg free, but instead it ended up being pulled off.

"I was still standing up," recalls Roger. "I didn't know what else to do so I started hopping towards the goal line. The referee ran over and threw his hands into the air. Touchdown! You know, even better than the six points was the look on the face of the other kid who was holding my artificial leg."

Roger's love of sports grew and so did his self-confidence. But not every obstacle gave way to Roger's determination. Eating in the lunchroom with the other kids watching him fumble with his food proved very painful to Roger, as did his repeated failure in typing class. "I learned a very good lesson from typing class," said Roger. "You can't do *everything* — it's better to concentrate on what you *can* do."

One thing Roger could do was swing a tennis racket. Unfortunately, when he swung it hard, his weak grip usually launched it into space. By luck, Roger stumbled upon an odd-looking tennis racket in a sports shop and accidentally wedged his finger between its double-barred handle when he picked it up. The snug fit made it possible for Roger to swing, serve and volley like an able-bodied player. He practiced every day and was soon playing — and losing — matches.

But Roger persisted. He practiced and practiced and played and played. Surgery on the two fingers of his left hand enabled Roger to grip his special racket better, greatly improving his game. Although he had no role models to guide him, Roger became obsessed with tennis and in time he started to win.

Roger went on to play college tennis, finishing his tennis career with 22 wins and 11 losses. He later became the first physically handicapped tennis player to be certified as a teaching professional by the United States Professional Tennis Association. Roger now tours the country, speaking to groups about what it takes to be a winner, no matter who you are.

"The only difference between you and me is that you can see my handicap, but I can't see yours. We *all* have them. When people ask me how I've been able to overcome my physical handicaps, I tell them that I haven't overcome anything. I've simply learned what I can't do — such as play the piano or eat with chopsticks — but more importantly, I've learned what I *can* do. Then I do what I can with all my heart and soul."

Jack Canfield

Yes, You Can

Experience is not what happens to a man. It is what a man does with what happens to him.

Aldous Huxley

What if at age 46 you were burned beyond recognition in a terrible motorcycle accident, and then four years later were paralyzed from the waist down in an airplane crash? Then, can you imagine yourself becoming a millionaire, a respected public speaker, a happy newlywed and a successful business person? Can you see yourself going white water rafting? Sky diving? Running for political office?

W. Mitchell has done all these things and more *after* two horrible accidents left his face a quilt of multicolored skin grafts, his hands fingerless and his legs thin and motionless in a wheelchair.

The 16 surgeries Mitchell endured after the motorcycle accident burned more than 65 percent of his body, left him unable to pick up a fork, dial a telephone or go to the bathroom without help. But Mitchell, a former Marine, never believed he was defeated. "I am in charge of my own spaceship," he said. "It's my up, my down. I could choose to see this situation as a setback or a starting point." Six months later he was piloting a plane again.

Mitchell bought himself a Victorian home in Colorado, some real estate, a plane and a bar. Later he teamed up with two friends and co-founded a wood burning stove company that grew to be Vermont's second largest private employer.

Then four years after the motorcycle accident, the plane Mitchell was piloting crashed back onto the runway during takeoff, crushing Mitchell's 12 thoracic vertebra and permanently paralyzing him from the waist down. "I wondered what was happening to me. What did I do to deserve this?"

Undaunted, Mitchell worked day and night to regain as much independence as possible. He was elected Mayor of Crested Butte, Colorado, to save the town from mineral mining that would ruin its beauty and environment. Mitchell later ran for Congress, turning his odd appearance into an asset with slogans such as, "Not just another pretty face."

Despite his initially shocking looks and physical challenges, Mitchell began white water rafting, he fell in love and married, earned a master's degree in public administration and continued flying, environmental activism and public speaking.

Mitchell's unshakable Positive Mental Attitude has earned him appearances on the "Today Show" and "Good Morning America" as well as feature articles in *Parade, Time, The New York Times* and other publications.

"Before I was paralyzed, there were 10,000 things I could do," Mitchell says. "Now there are 9,000. I can either dwell on the 1,000 I lost or focus on the 9,000 I have left. I tell people that I have had two big bumps in my life. If I have chosen not to use them as an excuse to quit, then maybe some of the experiences you are having which are pulling you back can be put into a new perspective. You can step back, take a wider view and have a chance to say, "Maybe that isn't such a big deal after all."

Remember: "It's not what happens to you, it's what you do about it."

Jack Canfield and Mark V. Hansen

Run, Patti, Run

At a young and tender age, Patti Wilson was told by her doctor that she was an epileptic. Her father, Jim Wilson, is a morning jogger. One day she smiled through her teenage braces and said, "Daddy what I'd really love to do is run with you every day, but I'm afraid I'll have a seizure."

Her father told her, "If you do, I know how to handle it so let's start running!"

That's just what they did every day. It was a wonderful experience for them to share and there were no seizures at all while she was running. After a few weeks, she told her father, "Daddy, what I'd really love to do is break the world's long-distance running record for women."

Her father checked the *Guiness Book of World Records* and found that the farthest any woman had run was 80 miles. As a freshman in high school, Patti announced, "I'm going to run from Orange County up to San Francisco." (A distance of 400 miles.) "As a sophomore," she went on, "I'm going to run to Portland, Oregon." (Over 1,500 miles.) "As a junior I'll run to St. Louis. (About 2,000 miles.) "As a senior I'll run to the White House." (More than 3,000 miles away.)

In view of her handicap, Patti was as ambitious as she was enthusiastic, but she said she looked at the handicap of being an epileptic as simply "an inconvenience." She focused not on what she had lost, but on what she had *left*.

That year she completed her run to San Francisco wearing a T-shirt that read, "I Love Epileptics." Her dad ran every mile at her side, and her mom, a nurse, followed in a motor home behind them in case anything went wrong.

In her sophomore year Patti's classmates got behind her. They built a giant poster that read, "Run, Patti, Run!" (This has since become her motto and the title of a book she has written.) On her second marathon, en route to Portland, she fractured a bone in her foot. A doctor told her she had to stop her run. He said, "I've got to put a cast on your ankle so that you don't sustain permanent damage."

"Doc, you don't understand," she said. "This isn't just a whim of mine, it's a magnificent obsession! I'm not just doing it for me, I'm doing it to break the chains on the brains that limit so many others. Isn't there a way I can keep running?" He gave her one option. He could wrap it in adhesive instead of putting it in a cast. He warned her that it would be incredibly painful, and he told her, "It will blister." She told the doctor to wrap it up.

She finished the run to Portland, completing her last mile with the governor of Oregon. You may have seen the headlines: "Super Runner, Patti Wilson Ends Marathon For Epilepsy On Her 17th Birthday."

After four months of almost continuous running from the West Coast to the East Coast, Patti arrived in Washington and shook the hand of the President of the United States. She told him, "I wanted people to know that epileptics are normal human beings with normal lives."

I told this story at one of my seminars not long ago, and afterward a big teary-eyed man came up to me, stuck out his big meaty hand and said, "Mark, my name is Jim Wilson. You were talking about my daughter, Patti." Because of her noble efforts, he told me, enough money had been raised to open up 19 multimillion-dollar epileptic centers around the country.

If Patti Wilson can do so much with so little, what can you do to outperform yourself in a state of total wellness?

Mark V. Hansen

The Power Of Determination

The little country schoolhouse was heated by an old-fashioned, pot-bellied coal stove. A little boy had the job of coming to school early each day to start the fire and warm the room before his teacher and his classmates arrived.

One morning they arrived to find the schoolhouse engulfed in flames. They dragged the unconscious little boy out of the flaming building more dead than alive. He had major burns over the lower half of his body and was taken to the nearby county hospital.

From his bed the dreadfully burned, semi-conscious little boy faintly heard the doctor talking to his mother. The doctor told his mother that her son would surely die — which was for the best, really — for the terrible fire had devastated the lower half of his body.

But the brave boy didn't want to die. He made up his mind that he would survive. Somehow, to the amazement of the physician, he did survive. When the mortal danger was past, he again heard the doctor and his mother speaking quietly. The mother was told that since the fire had destroyed so much flesh in the lower part of his body, it would almost be better if he had died, since he was doomed to be a lifetime cripple with no use at all of his lower limbs.

Once more the brave boy made up his mind. He would *not* be a cripple. He would walk. But unfortunately from the waist down, he had no motor ability. His thin legs just dangled there, all but lifeless.

Ultimately he was released from the hospital. Every day his mother would massage his little legs, but there was no feeling, no control, nothing. Yet his determination that he would walk was as strong as ever.

When he wasn't in bed, he was confined to a wheelchair. One sunny day his mother wheeled him out into the yard to get some fresh air. This day, instead of sitting there, he threw himself from the chair. He pulled himself across the grass, dragging his legs behind him.

He worked his way to the white picket fence bordering their lot. With great effort, he raised himself up on the fence. Then, stake by stake, he began dragging himself along the fence, resolved that he would walk. He started to do this every day until he wore a smooth path all around the yard beside the fence. There was nothing he wanted more than to develop life in those legs.

Ultimately through his daily massages, his iron persistence and his resolute determination, he did develop the ability to stand up, then to walk haltingly, then to walk by himself — and then — to run.

He began to walk to school, then to run to school, to run for the sheer joy of running. Later in college he made the track team.

Still later in Madison Square Garden this young man who was not expected to survive, who would surely never walk, who could never hope to run — this determined young man, Dr. Glenn Cunningham, ran the world's fastest mile!

Burt Dubin

The Power Of Optimism

The years of the Vietnam War were a confused troubled time for American foreign policy, making the suffering of the participants all the more tragic. But out of it has come the marvelous story about Captain Gerald L. Coffee.

His plane was shot down over the China Sea on February 3, 1966, and he spent the next seven years in a succession of prison camps. The POWs who survived, he says, did so by a regimen of physical exercise, prayer and stubborn communication with one another. After days of torture on the Vietnamese version of the rack, he signed the confession they demanded. Then he was thrown back into his cell to writhe in pain. Even worse was his guilt over having cracked. He did not know if there were other American prisoners in the cell block, but then he heard a voice: "Man in cell number 6 with the broken arm, can you hear me?"

It was Col. Robinson Risner. "It's safe to talk. Welcome to Heartbreak Hotel," he said.

"Colonel, any word about my navigator, Bob Hansen?" Coffee asked.

"No. Listen, Jerry, you must learn to communicate by tapping on the walls. It's the only dependable link we have to each other."

Risner had said "we"! That meant there were others. "Thank God, now I'm back with the others," Coffee thought.

"Have they tortured you, Jerry?" Risner asked.

"Yes. And I feel terrible that they got anything out of me."

"Listen," Risner said, "once they decide to break a man, they do it. The important thing is how you come back. Just follow the Code. Resist to the utmost of your ability. If they break you, just don't stay broken. Lick your wounds and bounce back. Talk to someone if you can. Don't get down on yourself. We need to take care of one another."

For days at a time Coffee would be punished for some minor infraction by being stretched on the ropes. His buddy in the next cell would tap on the wall, telling him to "hang tough," that he was praying for him. "Then, when he was being punished," Coffee says, "I would be on the wall doing the same for him."

At last Coffee received a letter from his wife:

> Dear Jerry,
>
> It has been a beautiful spring but of course we miss you. The kids are doing great. Kim skis all the way around the lake now. The boys swim and dive off the dock, and little Jerry splashes around with a plastic bubble on his back.

Coffee stopped reading because his eyes were filling with tears as he clutched his wife's letter to his chest. "Little Jerry? Who's Jerry?" Then he realized. Their baby, born after his imprisonment, had been a son and she had named him Jerry. There was no way she could know that all her previous letters had been undelivered, so she talked about their new son matter of-factly. Coffee says:

"Holding her letter, I was full of emotions: relief at finally knowing that the family was well, sorrow for missing out on Jerry's entire first year, gratitude for the blessing of simply being alive." The letter concluded:

> All of us, plus so many others, are praying for your safety and return soon. Take good care of yourself, honey.
>
> I love you.
>
> Bea

Coffee tells about the long, long hours during which the prisoners played movies in their minds, of going from room to room in their houses back home, the camera taking in every detail. Over and over they played scenes of what it was going to be like to be back. Coffee says it was his friends and his faith that helped him through. Every Sunday the senior officer in each cell block would pass a signal — church call. Every man stood up in his cell, if he was able, and then with a semblance of togetherness, they would recite the Twenty-Third Psalm: "Thou preparest a table before me in the presence of mine enemies, thou anointest my head with oil; my cup runneth over."

Coffee says: "I realized that despite being incarcerated in this terrible place, it was my cup that runneth over because someday, however, whenever, I would return to a beautiful and free country."

Finally, the peace treaty was signed, and on February 3, 1973, the seventh anniversary of his capture, Coffee was called before two young Vietnamese officers.

"Today it is our duty to return your belongings," one said.

"What belongings?" he asked.

"This."

He swallowed hard and reached for the gold wedding band the soldier held between his thumb and forefinger. Yes, it was his. He slipped it onto his finger. A little loose, but definitely his ring. He had never expected to see it again.

[My] kids were 11 or 12 years old when my ring had been taken away. Suddenly I felt old and weary. During the prime years of my life, I had sat in a medieval dungeon, had my arm screwed up, had contracted worms and God knows what else. I wondered if my children, now older and changed so much, would accept me back into the family and what our reunion would be like. And I thought of Bea. Would I be okay for her? Did she still love me? Could she possibly know how much she had meant to me all these years?

The bus trip to the Hanoi airport was a blur, but one thing stood out with clarity for Coffee: The bright beautiful, red, white, and blue flag painted on the tail of the enormous Air Force C-141 transport that gleamed in the sun, awaiting the first load of freed prisoners.

Next to the aircraft were several dozen American military people who smiled at them through the fence and gave them the thumbs-up signal. As they lined up by twos, the Vietnamese officer reeled off their names, rank and service.

"Commander Gerald L. Coffee, United States Navy," (He had been promoted two ranks in his absence.)

As Coffee stepped forward, his attention was riveted on an American colonel wearing crisp Air Force blues, wings and ribbons. It was the first American military uniform he had seen in many years. The colonel returned Coffee's brisk salute.

"Commander Gerald L. Coffee reporting for duty, sir."

"Welcome back, Jerry." The colonel reached forward with both hands and shook Coffee's hand. When the plane was loaded, the pilot taxied directly onto the runway without holding short, then locked the brakes and jammed his throttles forward. The huge beast rocked and vibrated as the pilot made his final checks of the engine's performance. The roar was horrendous as the brakes were released and they lurched forward on the runway. When they were airborne, the pilot's voice came onto the speaker and filled the cabin. It was a strong, sure voice.

"Congratulations, gentlemen. We've just left North Vietnam." Only then did they erupt into cheers.

The first leg of their trip home took them to Clark Air Force Base in the Philippines. The crowd held up banners: "Welcome Home! We love you. God bless." From behind the security lines they applauded wildly as the name of each debarking POW was announced. There were television cameras, but the men had no idea that at that very moment in the small hours of the morning, millions of Americans back home were riveted to their television sets, cheering and weeping.

Special telephones had been set up to accommodate their initial calls home. Coffee's stomach churned as he waited the interminable few seconds for Bea to pick up the phone in Sanford, Florida, where she and the children were waiting.

"Hello, babe. It's me. Can you believe it?"

"Hi, honey. Yes. We watched you on TV when you came off the airplane. I think everybody in America saw you. You look great!"

"I dunno. I'm kinda scrawny. But I'm okay. I'm just anxious to get home."

After his long-awaited reunion with his wife and children, he and his family attended mass the following Sunday. Afterwards, in response to the parish priest's welcome, here is what Coffee said. It summarizes as well as anything I know of the optimist's code:

> Faith was really the key to my survival all those years. Faith in myself to simply pursue my duty to the best of my ability and ultimately return home with honor. Faith in my fellow man, starting with all of you here, knowing you would be looking out for my family, and faith in my comrades in those various cells and cell blocks in prison, men upon whom I depended and who in turn depended upon me, sometimes desperately. Faith in my country, its institutions and our national purpose and cause . . . And, of course, faith in God — truly, as all of you know, the foundation for it all . . . Our lives are a continuing journey — and we must learn and grow at every bend as we make our way, sometimes stumbling, but always moving, toward the finest within us.

David McNally

From The Power of Optimism
by Alan Loy McGinnis

Faith

We're a rugged breed, us quads. If we weren't, we wouldn't be around today. Yes, we're a rugged breed. In many ways, we've been blessed with a savvy and spirit that isn't given to everybody.

And let me say that this refusal of total or full acceptance of one's disability all hooks up with one thing — faith, an almost divine faith.

Down in the reception room of the Institute of Physical Medicine and Rehabilitation, over on the East River at 400 East 34th Street in New York City, there's a bronze plaque that's riveted to the wall. During the months of coming back to the Institute for treatment — two or three times a week — I rolled through that reception room many times, coming and going. But I never quite made the time to pull over to one side and read the words on that plaque that were written, it's said, by an unknown Confederate soldier. Then one afternoon, I did. I read it and then I read it again. When I finished it for the second time, I was near to bursting — not in despair, but with an inner glow that had me straining to grip the arms of my wheelchair. I'd like to share it with you.

A Creed For Those Who Have Suffered

I asked God for strength, that I might achieve.
I was made weak, that I might learn humbly to obey . . .

I asked for health, that I might do great things.
I was given infirmity, that I might do better things . . .

I asked for riches, that I might be happy.
I was given poverty, that I might be wise . . .

I asked for power, that I might have the praise of men.
I was given weakness, that I might feel the need of God . . .

I asked for all things, that I might enjoy life.
I was given life, that I might enjoy all things . . .

I got nothing I asked for — but everything I had hoped for.

Almost despite myself, my unspoken prayers were answered.

I am, among men, most richly blessed!

Roy Campanella

She Saved 219 Lives

Mrs. Betty Tisdale is a world-class heroine. When the war in Vietnam heated up back in April of 1975, she knew she had to save the 400 orphans who were about to be put on the streets. She had already adopted five orphaned Vietnamese girls with her former pediatrician husband, Col. Patrick Tisdale, who was a widower and already had five children.

As a U.S. Naval doctor in Vietnam in 1954, Tom Dooley had helped refugees flee from the communist north. Betty says, "I really feel Tom Dooley was a saint. His influence changed my life forever." Because of Dooley's book, she took her life savings and traveled to Vietnam 14 times on her vacations to visit and work in the hospitals and orphanages he had founded. While in Saigon, she fell in love with the orphans at An Lac (Happy Place), run by Madame Vu Thi Ngai, who was later evacuated by Betty the day Vietnam fell, and returned with her to Georgia to live with Betty and her ten children.

When Betty, a do-it-now and invent-solutions-as-problems-arise kind of person, realized the 400 children's plight, she went into warp speed action. She called Madame Ngai and said, "Yes! I'll come and get the children and get them all adopted." She didn't know how she would do it. She just knew that she'd do it. Later, in a movie of the evacuation, "The Children of An Lac," Shirley Jones portrayed Betty.

In moments she began to move mountains. She raised the necessary money in many different ways, even including accepting green stamps. She simply decided to do it and she did it. She said, "I visualized all those babies growing up in good Christian homes in America, not under communism." That kept her motivated.

She left for Vietnam from Fort Benning, Georgia, on Sunday, arrived on Tuesday in Saigon, and miraculously and sleeplessly conquered every obstacle to airlift 400 children out of Saigon by Saturday morning. However, upon her arrival, the head of Vietnam's social welfare, Dr. Dan, suddenly announced he would only approve children under ten years old and all the children must have birth certificates. She quickly discovered war orphans are fortunate to simply be alive. They don't have birth certificates.

Betty went to the hospital pediatric department, obtained 225 birth certificates, and quickly created birth dates, times and places for the 219 eligible babies, toddlers and youngsters. She says, "I have no idea when, where and to whom they were born. My fingers just created birth certificates." Birth certificates were the only hope they had to depart the place safely and have a viable future with freedom. It was now or never.

Now she needed a place to house the orphans once they were evacuated . . . The military at Ft. Benning resisted, but Betty brilliantly and tenaciously persisted. Try as she might, she could not get the Commanding General on the phone, so she called the office of the Secretary of the Army, Bo Callaway. His duty, too, was not answering Betty's calls, no matter how urgent and of life-saving importance they were.

However, Betty was not to be beaten. She had come too far and done too much to be stopped now. So since he was from Georgia, she called his mother and pleaded her case. Betty enrolled her with her heart and asked her to intercede. Virtually overnight, the Secretary of the Army, her son, responded and arranged that a school at Ft. Benning be used as the interim home for the orphans of An Lac.

But the challenge of how to get the children OUT was still to be accomplished. When Betty arrived in Saigon, she went to Ambassador Graham Martin immediately and pleaded for some sort of transportation for the children. She had tried to charter a Pan Am plane, but Lloyds of London had raised the insurance so high that it was impossible to negotiate at this time. The Ambassador agreed to help if all the papers were cleared through the Vietnamese government. Dr. Dan signed the last manifest, literally, as the children were boarding the two airforce planes.

The orphans were malnourished and sickly. Most had never been away from the orphanage. They were scared. She had recruited soldiers and the ABC crew to help strap them in, transport them and feed them. You can't believe how deeply and permanently those volunteers' hearts were touched that beautiful Saturday as 219 children were transported to freedom. Every volunteer cried with joy and appreciation that they had tangibly contributed to another's freedom.

Chartering airlines home from the Philippines was a huge hassle. There was a $21,000 expense for a United Airlines plane. Dr. Tisdale guaranteed payment because of his love for the orphans. Had Betty had more time, she could have probably got it for free! But time was a factor so she moved quickly.

Every child was adopted within one month of arriving in the United States. The Tressler Lutheran

Agency in York, Pennsylvania, which specializes in getting handicapped children adopted, found a home for each orphan.

Betty has proven over and over again that you can do anything at all if you are simply willing to ask, to not settle for a "no," to do whatever it takes and to persevere.

As Dr. Tom Dooley once said, "It takes ordinary people to do extraordinary things."

Jack Canfield and Mark V. Hansen

Are You Going To Help Me?

In 1989 an 8.2 earthquake almost flattened Armenia, killing over 30,000 people in less than four minutes.

In the midst of utter devastation and chaos, a father left his wife securely at home and rushed to the school where his son was supposed to be, only to discover that the building was as flat as a pancake.

After the traumatic initial shock, he remembered the promise he had made to his son: "No matter what, I'll always be there for you!" And tears began to fill his eyes. As he looked at the pile of debris that once was the school, it looked hopeless, but he kept remembering his commitment to his son.

He began to concentrate on where he walked his son to class at school each morning. Remembering his son's classroom would be in the back right corner of the building, he rushed there and started digging through the rubble.

As he was digging, other forlorn parents arrived, clutching their hearts, saying: "My son!" "My daughter!" Other well meaning parents tried to pull him off of what was left of the school saying:

"It's too late!"

"They're dead!"

"You can't help!"

"Go home!"

"Come on, face reality, there's nothing you can do!"

"You're just going to make things worse!"

To each parent he responded with one line: "Are you going to help me now?" And then he proceeded to dig for his son, stone by stone.

The fire chief showed up and tried to pull him off of the school's debris saying "Fires are breaking out, explosions are happening everywhere. You're in danger. We'll take care of it. Go home." To which this loving, caring Armenian father asked, "Are you going to help me now?"

The police came and said, "You're angry, distraught and it's over. You're endangering others. Go home. We'll handle it!" To which he replied, "Are you going to help me now?" No one helped.

Courageously he proceeded alone because he needed to know for himself: "Is my boy alive or is he dead?"

He dug for eight hours . . . 12 hours . . . 24 hours . . . 36 hours . . . then, in the 38th hour, he pulled back a boulder and heard his son's voice. He screamed his son's name, *"ARMAND!"* He heard back, "Dad!?! It's me, Dad! I told the other kids not to worry. I told 'em that if you were alive, you'd save me and when you saved me, they'd be saved. You promised, 'No matter what, I'll always be there for you!' You did it, Dad!"

"What's going on in there? How is it?" the father asked.

"There are 14 of us left out of 33, Dad. We're scared, hungry, thirsty and thankful you're here. When the building collapsed, it made a wedge, like a triangle, and it saved us."

"Come on out, boy!"

"No, Dad! Let the other kids out first, 'cause I know you'll get me! No matter what, I know you'll be there for me!"

Mark V. Hansen

Just One More Time

There's a 19th-century English novel set in a small Welsh town in which every year for the past 500 years the people all gather in church on Christmas Eve and pray. Shortly before midnight, they light candle lanterns and, singing carols and hymns, they walk down a country path several miles to an old abandoned stone shack. There they set up a creche scene, complete with manger. And in simple piety, they kneel and pray. Their hymns warm the chilly December air. Everyone in town capable of walking is there.

There is a myth in that town, a belief that if all citizens are present on Christmas Eve, and if all are praying with perfect faith, then and only then, at the stroke of midnight, the Second Coming will be at hand. And for 500 years they've come to that stone ruin and prayed. Yet the Second Coming has eluded them.

One of the main characters in this novel is asked, "Do you believe that He will come again on Christmas Eve in our town?"

"No," he answers, shaking his head sadly, "no, I don't."

"Then why do you go each year?" he asked.

"Ah," he says smiling, "what if I were the only one who wasn't there when it happened?"

Well, that's very little faith he has, isn't it? But it is some faith. As it says in the New Testament, we need only have faith as small as a grain of mustard seed to get into the Kingdom of Heaven. And sometimes, when we work with disturbed children, at-risk youth, troubled teens, alcoholic or abusive or depressed and suicidal partners, friends or clients . . . it is at those moments that we need that small bit of faith that kept that man coming back to the stone ruin on Christmas Eve. Just one more time. Just this next time, perhaps I'll make the breakthrough then.

We sometimes are called upon to work with people for whom others have abandoned all hope. Perhaps we have even come to the conclusion that there's no possibility of change or growth. It's at that time that, if we can find the tiniest scrap of hope, we may turn the corner, achieve a measurable gain, save someone worth saving. Please go back, my friend, just this one more time.

Hanoch McCarty

There Is Greatness All Around You — Use It

There are many people who could be Olympic champions, All-Americans who have never tried. I'd estimate five million people could have beaten me in the pole vault the years I won it, at *least* five million. Men who were stronger, bigger and faster than I was could have done it, but they never picked up a pole, never made the feeble effort to pick their legs off the ground to try to get over the bar.

Greatness is all around us. It's easy to be great because great people will help you. What is fantastic about all the conventions I go to is that the greatest in the business will come and share their ideas, their methods and their techniques with everyone else. I have seen the greatest salesmen open up and show young salesmen exactly how they did it. They don't hold back. I have also found it true in the world of sports.

I'll never forget the time I was trying to break Dutch Warmer Dam's record. I was about a foot below his record, so I called him on the phone. I said, "Dutch, can you help me? I seem to have leveled off. I can't get any higher."

He said, "Sure, Bob, come on up to visit me and I'll give you all I got." I spent three days with the master, the greatest pole vaulter in the world. For three days, Dutch gave me everything that he'd seen. There were things that I was doing wrong and he corrected them. To make a long story short, I went up eight inches. That great guy gave me the best that he had. I've found that sports champions and heroes willingly do this just to help you become great, too.

John Wooden, the great UCLA basketball coach, has a philosophy that every day he is supposed to help someone who can never reciprocate. That's his obligation.

When in college working on his masters thesis on scouting and defensive football, George Allen wrote up a 30-page survey and sent it out to the great coaches in the country. Eighty-five percent answered it completely.

Great people will share, which is what made George Allen one of the greatest football coaches in the world. Great people will tell you their secrets. Look for them, call them on the phone or buy their books. Go where they are, get around them, talk to them. It is easy to be great when you get around great people.

Bob Richards
Olympic Athlete

7

ECLECTIC WISDOM

This life is a test.
It is only a test.
Had it been an actual life
You would have received
Further instructions on
Where to go and what to do!

Found on a bulletin board

You've Got Yourself A Deal!

When Marita was 13, it was the era of tie-dyed T-shirts and frayed jeans. Even though I had grown up in the Depression and had no money for clothes, I had never dressed this poorly. One day I saw her out in the driveway rubbing the hems of her new jeans with dirt and rocks. I was aghast at her ruining these pants I had just paid for and ran out to tell her so. She continued to grind on as I recounted my soap opera of childhood deprivation. As I concluded without having moved her to tears of repentance, I asked why she was wrecking her new jeans. She replied without looking up, "You can't wear new ones."

"Why not?"

"You just can't, so I'm messing them up to make them look old." Such total loss of logic! How could it be the style to ruin new clothes?

Each morning as she would leave for school I would stare at her and sigh, "My daughter looking like that." There she'd stand in her father's old T-shirt, tie-dyed with big blue spots and streaks. Fit for a duster, I thought. And those jeans — so low-slung I feared if she took a deep breath, they'd drop off her rear. But where would they go? They were so tight and stiff they couldn't move. The frayed bottoms, helped by the rocks, had strings that dragged behind her as she walked.

One day after she had left for school, it was as if the Lord got my attention and said, "Do you realize what your last words are to Marita each morning? 'My daughter looking like that.' When she gets to school and her friends talk about their old-fashioned mothers who complain all the time, she'll have your constant comments to contribute. Have you ever looked at the other girls in junior high? Why not give them a glance?"

I drove over to pick her up that day and observed that many of the other girls looked even worse. On the way home I mentioned how I had over-reacted to her ruining her jeans. I offered a compromise: "From now on you can wear anything you want to school and with your friends, and I won't bug you about it."

"That'll be a relief."

"But when I take you out with me to church or shopping or to my friends, I'd like you to dress in something you know I like without my having to say a word."

She thought about it.

Then I added, "That means you get 95 percent your way and I get 5 percent for me. What do you think?"

She got a twinkle in her eye as she put out her hand and shook mine. "Mother, you've got yourself a deal!"

From then on I gave her a happy farewell in the morning and didn't bug her about her clothes. When I took her out with me, she dressed properly without fussing. We had ourselves a deal!

Florence Littauer

Take A Moment To Really See

We have all heard the expression: "Remember to stop and smell the roses." But, how often do we really take time out of our hectic fast-paced lives to notice the world around us? Too often we get caught up in our busy schedules, thoughts of our next appointment, the traffic or life in general, to even realize there are other people nearby.

I am as guilty as anyone of tuning out the world in this manner, especially when I am driving on California's overcrowded streets. A short time ago, however, I witnessed an event that showed me how being wrapped up in my own little world has kept me from being fully aware of the bigger world picture around me.

I was driving to a business appointment and, as usual, I was planning in my mind what I was going to say. I came to a very busy intersection where the stoplight had just turned red. "All right," I thought to myself, "I can beat the next light if I race ahead of the pack."

My mind and car were in auto pilot, ready to go when suddenly my trance was broken by an unforgettable sight. A young couple, both blind, were walking arm-in-arm across this busy intersection with cars whizzing by in every direction. The man was holding the hand of a little boy, while the woman was clutching a baby sling to her chest, obviously carrying a child. Each of them had a white cane extended, searching for clues to navigate them across the intersection.

Initially I was moved. They were overcoming what I felt was one of the most feared handicaps — blindness. "Wouldn't it be terrible to be blind?" I thought. My thought was quickly interrupted by horror when I saw that the couple were not walking in the crosswalk, but were instead veering diagonally, directly toward the middle of the intersection. Without realizing the danger they were in, they were walking right smack into the path of oncoming cars. I was frightened for them because I didn't know if the other drivers understood what was happening.

As I watched from the front line of traffic (I had the best seat in the house), I saw a miracle unfold before my eyes. *Every* car in *every* direction came to a simultaneous stop. I never heard the screech of brakes or even the peep of a car horn. Nobody even yelled, "Get out of the way!" Everything froze. In that moment, time seemed to stand still for this family.

Amazed, I looked at the cars around me to verify that we were all seeing the same thing. I noticed that everyone's attention was also fixed on the couple. Suddenly the driver to my right reacted. Craning his head out of his car, he yelled, "To your right. To your right!" Other people followed in unison, shouting, "To your right!"

Never skipping a beat, the couple adjusted their course as they followed the coaching. Trusting their white canes and the calls from some concerned citizens, they made it to the other side of the road. As they arrived at the curb, one thing struck me — they were still arm-in-arm.

I was taken aback by the emotionless expressions on their faces and judged that they had no idea what was really going on around them. Yet I immediately sensed the sighs of relief exhaled by everyone stopped at that intersection.

As I glanced into the cars around me, the driver on my right was mouthing the words "Whew, did you see that?!" The driver to the left of me was saying, "I can't believe it!" I think all of us were deeply moved by what we had just witnessed. Here were human beings stepping outside themselves for a moment to help four people in need.

I have reflected back on this situation many times since it happened and have learned several powerful lessons from it. The first is: "Slow down and smell the roses." (Something I had rarely done up until then.) Take time to look around and really *see* what is going on in front of you right now. Do this and you will realize that this moment is all there is, more importantly, this moment is all that you have to make a difference in life.

The second lesson I learned is that the goals we set for ourselves can be attained through faith in ourselves and trust in others, despite seemingly insurmountable obstacles.

The blind couple's goal was simply to get to the other side of the road intact. Their obstacle was eight lines of cars aimed straight at them. Yet, without panic or doubt, they walked forward until they reached their goal.

We too can move forward in attaining our goals, putting blinders on to the obstacles that would stand in our way. We just need to trust our intuition and accept the guidance of others who may have greater insight.

Finally, I learned to really appreciate my gift of sight, something I had taken for granted all too often.

Can you imagine how different life would be without your eyes? Try to imagine for a moment, walking into a busy intersection without being able to see. How often we forget the simple yet incredible gifts we have in our life.

As I drove away from that busy intersection, I did so with more awareness of life and compassion for others than I had arrived there with. Since then I have made the decision to really see life as I go about my daily activities and use my God-given talents to help others less fortunate.

Do yourself a favor as you walk through life: Slow down and take the time to really *see.* Take a moment to see what is going on around you right now, right where you are. You may be missing something wonderful.

J. Michael Thomas

If I Had My Life To Live Over

Interviews with the elderly and the terminally ill do not report that people have regret for the things they have done but rather people talk about the things they regret not having done.

I'd dare to make more mistakes next time.
I'd relax. I would limber up.
I would be sillier than I have been this trip.
I would take fewer things seriously.
I would take more chances.
I would take more trips.
I would climb more mountains and swim more rivers.
I would eat more ice cream and less beans.
I would perhaps have more actual troubles but I'd have fewer imaginary ones.
You see, I'm one of those people who live sensibly and sanely hour after hour, day after day.
Oh, I've had my moments and if I had it to do over again, I'd have more of them. In fact, I'd try to have nothing else. Just moments.
One after another, instead of living so many years ahead of each day.

I've been one of those people who never go anywhere without a thermometer, a hot water bottle, a raincoat and a parachute.

If I had it to do again, I would travel lighter next time.

If I had my life to live over, I would start barefoot earlier in the spring and stay that way later in the fall.
I would go to more dances.
I would ride more merry-go-rounds.
I would pick more daisies.

Nadine Stair
(age 85)

Two Monks

Two monks on a pilgrimage came to the ford of a river. There they saw a girl dressed in all her finery, obviously not knowing what to do since the river was high and she did not want to spoil her clothes. Without more ado, one of the monks took her on his back, carried her across and put her down on dry ground on the other side.

Then the monks continued on their way. But the other monk after an hour started complaining, "Surely it is not right to touch a woman; it is against the commandments to have close contact with women. How could you go against the rules of monks?"

The monk who had carried the girl walked along silently, but finally he remarked, "I set her down by the river an hour ago, why are you still carrying her?"

Irmgard Schloegl
The Wisdom of Zen Masters

Sachi

Soon after her brother was born, little Sachi began to ask her parents to leave her alone with the new baby. They worried that like most four-year-olds, she might feel jealous and want to hit or shake him, so they said no. But she showed no signs of jealousy. She treated the baby with kindness and her pleas to be left alone with him became more urgent. They decided to allow it.

Elated, she went into the baby's room and shut the door, but it opened a crack — enough for her curious parents to peek in and listen. They saw little Sachi walk quietly up to her baby brother, put her face close to his and say quietly, "Baby, tell me what God feels like. I'm starting to forget."

Dan Millman

The Dolphin's Gift

I was in about 40 feet of water, alone. I knew I should not have gone alone, but I was very competent and just took a chance. There was not much current, and the water was so warm, clear and enticing. When I got a cramp, I realized at once how foolish I was. I was not too alarmed, but *was* completely doubled up with stomach cramps. I tried to remove my weight belt, but I was so doubled up I could not get to the catch. I was sinking and began to feel more frightened, unable to move. I could see my watch and knew there was only a little more time on the tank before I would be out of air. I tried to massage my abdomen. I wasn't wearing a wet suit, but couldn't straighten out and couldn't get to the cramped muscles with my hands.

I thought, "I can't go like this! I have things to do!" I just couldn't die anonymously this way with no one to even know what happened to me. I called out in my mind, "Somebody, something, help me!"

I was not prepared for what happened. Suddenly I felt a prodding from behind me under the armpit. I thought, "Oh no, sharks!" I felt real terror and despair. But my arm was being lifted forcibly. Around into my field of vision came an eye — the most marvelous eye I could ever imagine. I swear it was smiling. It was the eye of a big dolphin. Looking into that eye, I knew I was safe.

It moved farther forward, nudging under and hooking its dorsal fin below my armpit with my arm over its back. I relaxed, hugging it, flooded with relief. I felt that the animal was conveying security to me, that it was healing me as well as lifting me toward the surface. My stomach cramps went away as we ascended and I relaxed with security, but I felt very strongly that it healed me too.

At the surface it drew me all the way into shore. It took me into water so shallow that I began to be concerned that it might be beached, and I pushed it back a little deeper, where it waited, watching me, I guess to see if I was all right.

It felt like another lifetime. When I took off the weight belt and oxygen tank, I just took everything off and went naked back into the ocean to the dolphin. I felt so light and free and alive, and just wanted to play in the sun and the water in all that freedom. The dolphin took me back out and played around in the water with me. I noticed that there were a lot of dolphins there, farther out.

After a while it brought me back to shore. I was very tired then, almost collapsing and he made sure I was safe in the shallowest water. Then he turned sideways with one eye looking into mine. We stayed that way for what seemed like a very long time, timeless I guess, in a trance almost, with personal thoughts from the past going through my mind. Then he made just one sound and went out to join the others. And all of them left.

Elizabeth Gawain

The Touch Of The Master's Hand

'Twas battered and scarred, and the auctioneer
Thought it scarcely worth his while
To waste much time on the old violin,
But held it up with a smile.
"What am I bidden, good folks," he cried,
"Who'll start the bidding for me?"
"A dollar, a dollar," then, two! Only two?
"Two dollars, and who'll make it three?
"Three dollars, once; three dollars, twice;
Going for three . . ." But no,
From the room, far back, a grey-haired man
Came forward and picked up the bow;
Then, wiping the dust from the old violin,
And tightening the loose strings,
He played a melody pure and sweet
As a caroling angel sings.

The music ceased, and the auctioneer,
With a voice that was quiet and low,
Said: "What am I bid for the old violin?"
And he held it up with the bow.
"A thousand dollars, and who'll make it two?
Two thousand! And who'll make it three?
Three thousand, once; three thousand, twice;
And going and gone," said he.

The people cheered, but some of them cried,
"We do not quite understand
What changed its worth?" Swift came the reply:
"The touch of a master's hand."

And many a man with life out of tune,
And battered and scarred with sin,
Is auctioned cheap to the thoughtless crowd,
Much like the old violin.
A "mess of potage," a glass of wine;
A game — and he travels on.
He is "going" once, and "going" twice,
He's "going" and almost "gone."
But the Master comes and the foolish crowd
Never can quite understand
The worth of a soul and the change that's wrought
By the touch of the Master's hand.

Myra B. Welch

More Chicken Soup?

Share your heart with the rest of the world. If you have a story, poem or article (your own or someone else's) that you feel belongs in a future volume of *Chicken Soup For The Soul,* please send it to us.

Jack Canfield and Mark Victor Hansen
Self-Esteem Seminars
6035 Bristol Parkway
Culver City, California 90230
FAX: 310-337-7465

We will make sure that you and the author are credited for the contribution. Thank you!

Lectures, Seminars And Workshops

You can also contact us at the above address for speaking engagements or for information about our newsletters, other books, audio tapes, workshops and training programs.

We wish you much love!
Jack and Mark

Contributors

Many of the stories in this book were taken from books we have read. These sources are acknowledged in the Acknowledgments section. Some of the stories and poems were contributed by friends of ours, who, like us, are professional speakers. If you would like to contact them for information on their books, tapes and seminars, you can reach them at the addresses and phone numbers provided below.

Wally "Famous" Amos is the founder of Famous Amos Cookies and author of the book and cassette album *The Power . . . In You*. Wally resides in Maui, Hawaii. He can be reached by writing to P.O. Box 897, Kailua, HI 96734 or call (808) 261-6075.

Joe Batten, C.P.A.E., is a professional speaker and a successful businessperson who knows how to inspire confidence in organizations in good economic times and bad. His 35 years as an author, consultant and speaker have earned him the title of Corporate Mentor. Joe wrote the best-selling book: *Tough Minded Management*. Joe is a man who loves life and laughter and translates that warmth and passion to every audience. You can reach Joe by writing to 2413 Grand Avenue, Des Moines, Iowa 50312 or call (515) 244-3176.

Gene Bedley is the principal of El Rancho Elementary School in Irvine, California, recipient of the PTA's 1985 National Educator of the Year Award and author of numerous books on creating a positive classroom environment. He can be reached at 14252 East Mall, Irvine, California 92714 or call (714) 551-3090.

Michele Borba is a prolific author on building self-esteem in elementary classrooms. She is a member of the board of trustees of the National Council for Self-Esteem. Her best book is *Esteem Builders,* a collection of 379 classroom activities. You can reach her by writing 840 Prescott Drive, Palm Springs, California 92262 or call (619) 323-5387.

Helice Bridges is a recognized and dynamic speaker and trainer who travels internationally doing self-esteem training and workshops for schools, organizations and businesses. She is Chairperson of the Board for Difference Makers, Inc. and can be reached at P.O. Box 2115, Del Mar, California 92014 or call (619) 481-6019.

Les Brown is a highly acclaimed speaker who talks to Fortune 500 companies and conducts personal and professional seminars around the country. He is well known to television audiences through his PBS specials, all of which are available on audiocassette and videotape. He can be reached by writing Les Brown Unlimited, 2180 Penobscot Building, Detroit, Michigan 48226 or call (800) 733-4226.

Dan Clark is a professional motivational speaker who has conducted thousands of talks for high school students, parents and corporations. He can be reached at P.O. Box 8689, Salt Lake City, Utah 84108 or call (801) 532-5755.

Alan Cohen is a proflific and dynamic speaker and author. Our favorite book of his is *The Dragon Doesn't Live Here Anymore.* He can be reached at P.O. Box 98509, Des Moines, WA 98198 or call (800) 462-3013.

Roger Crawford is a dynamic motivational speaker. His book is entitled *Playing From The Heart.* He can be reached by writing 1050 St. Andrews Drive, Byron, California 94514 or call (510) 634-8519.

Stan Dale, formerly the voice of "The Shadow" and the announcer/narrator of "The Lone Ranger," "Sgt. Preston" and "The Green Hornet" radio shows, is the Director/Founder of the Human Awareness Institute in San Mateo, California, an organization dedicated to "creating a world where everyone wins." He conducts "Sex, Love and Intimacy Workshops" around the world. Stan is the author of *Fantasies Can Set You Free* and *My Child, My Self: How To Raise The Child You Always Wanted To Be.* Both books are also available on cassette from The Human Awareness Institute, 1720 S. Amphlett Blvd., Suite 128, San Mateo, California 94402 or call (800) 800-4117 or (415) 571-5524.

Burt Dubin is the developer of the Speaking Success System, a powerful instrument for helping aspiring speakers develop platform presence and marketing magic. A specialist in marketing and positioning, Burt translates his skills from the platform when he addresses retail and wholesale associations and organizations. He can be reached at the Management Achievement Institute, Box 6543, Kingman, Arizona 86402-6543 or call (800) 321-1225.

Patricia Fripp, C.S.P., C.P.A.E., is a "speaker for all reasons." She is past president of the National Speakers Association and is one of the most dynamic speakers we know. She can be reached at 527 Hugo Street, San Francisco, California 94122 or call (415) 753-6556.

Bobbie Gee, C.S.P., is recognized as one of America's most outstanding female speakers. She is the author of the book *Winning the Image Game* (Pagemill Press) and two cassette albums *Life Doesn't Have To Be A Struggle* and *Image Power.* You can contact her at Bobbie Gee Enterprises, 1540 S. Coast Highway, Suite 206, Laguna Beach, California 92651 or call (800) 462-4386 or (714) 497-1915.

Rick Gelinas is the President of the Lucky Acorns Delphi Foundation in Miami, Florida. He is a master educator and has dedicated his life to making a difference to children. You can reach him at 5888 S.W. 77 Terrace, Miami, Florida 33143 or call (305) 667-7756.

John Goddard is an adventurer, explorer and world class motivational speaker. He can be reached at 4224 Beulah Drive, La Canada, California 91101 or call (818) 790-7094.

Patty Hansen is Mark's wife and is Administrative Director of Look Who's Talking. She can be reached at P.O. Box 7665, Newport Beach, California 92658 or call (714) 759-9304.

Danielle Kennedy, M.A., is a celebrated author, world class sales trainer, inspirationalist and award-winning saleswoman. She holds an Honorary Degree in the Humanities from Clarke College and a Masters in Professional Writing from the University of Southern California. She lectures in 100 cities a year on sales, marketing and leadership. Her best-selling books include *How To List And Sell Real Estate In The '90s* (Prentice Hall) and *Kennedy On Doubling Your Income In Real Estate Sales* (John Wiley). She is married and has eight children. She can be reached at 219 S. El Camino Real, San Clemente, California 92672 or call (714) 498-8033.

Florence Littauer, C.S.P., C.P.A.E., is one of the most wonderful people we know. She is an inspiring writer and teacher. Our favorite book of hers is *Little Silver Boxes.* She can be reached at 1645 Rancho Fe Rd., San Marcos, California 92069 or call (619) 744-9202.

Rick Little over the last 16 years has participated in a wide range of efforts to improve the social and economic conditions of children and youth. In 1975 he founded Quest International and served as its president for 15 years. Mr. Little has co-authored books with leading authorities on youth including Bill Cosby and Dr. Charlie W. Shedd. In 1990 Rick Little founded the International Youth Foundation with major support from the W.K. Kellogg Foundation. He now serves as Secretary General to the International Youth Foundation, whose goal is to identify and fund replicable youth programs which have demonstrated success. The foundation currently focuses on programs in Southern Africa, Poland, Ecuador, Mexico, Bangladesh, Thailand and the Philippines.

Hanoch McCarty, Ed.D., is a professional speaker, trainer and consultant specializing in motivation, productivity and self-esteem enhancement. Hanoch is one of the most sought-after speakers in the nation because he combines humor and moving stories with practical skills that can be put to work immediately. His books and video tape programs include *Stress and Energy* and *Self-Esteem: The Bottom Line.* He can be reached at P.O. Box 66, Galt, California 95632 or call (800) 231-7353.

Dan Millman is the author of inspirational books for adults and children. He is a past world champion gymnast, university coach and college professor whose disillusion with "the usual life" sent him around the world and into the depths of his mind and heart. His experiences generated an approach to life he calls "the way of the peaceful warrior." His books include *Way of the Peaceful Warrior, The Warrior Athlete* and *No Ordinary Moments.*

He can be reached at Peaceful Warrior Services, P.O. Box 6148, San Rafael, California 94903 or call (415) 491-0301.

W. Mitchell, C.P.A.E., is one of the most inspirational speakers we have ever met. His tape program is entitled *It's Not What Happens To You, It's What You Do About It.* He can be reached at 12014 W. 54th Drive, #100, Arvada, Colorado 80002 or call (303) 425-1800.

Robert A. Moawad is Chairman and Chief Executive Officer of Edge Learning Institute with offices in Tacoma, Washington, and Tempe, Arizona. Edge is a professional development firm dedicated to assisting organizations achieve greater levels of productivity, quality and customer satisfaction. Bob is a dynamic "edu-tainer." He has an impressive ability to inspire and have an impact on an audience by blending colorful illustrations with solid principles. This has made Bob one of the most sought-after keynote speakers in the nation. Since 1973 he has assisted more than two million people, including some of the most respected leaders in business, government and education. He can be contacted by writing Edge Learning Institute, 2217 N. 30th, #200, Tacoma, Washington 98403 or call (206) 272-3103.

Chick Moorman is the director of the Institute for Personal Power, a consulting firm dedicated to providing high-quality professional development activities for educators and parents. Every year he crisscrosses the country conducting over 100 workshops on cooperative learning, enhancing self-esteem and developing positive attitudes. His mission is to help people experience a greater sense of personal power in their lives so they can in turn empower others. His latest book, co-authored with his wife, Nancy, is *Teacher Talk: What it Really Means. Teacher Talk* explores the way teachers talk to children and examines the underlying "silent messages" that accompany the spoken word. It can be ordered at $11.95 from The Institute for Personal Power, P.O. Box 1130, Bay City, Michigan 48706 or call (517) 686-3251.

Michael Murphy, Ed.D., is a forensic psychologist, newspaper columnist, teacher and Family Consultation Team member. Write to him at 25 Monument Rd., Orleans, MA 02653 or call (508) 255-4050.

Victor H. Nelson, S.T.M., is a therapist and pastoral counselor in private practice. His address is 505 Evergreen Street West, Lafayette, Indiana 47906.

Price Pritchett, Ph.D., holds a doctorate in psychology and is past president of the Dallas Psychological Association. He is the CEO of Pritchett & Associates, Inc., a Dallas-based consulting firm specializing in organizational change. Dr. Pritchett has authored 11 books on individual and organizational effectiveness, including *You:^{2}: A High Velocity Formula For Multiplying Your Personal Effectiveness In Quantum Leaps*. You can contact Dr. Pritchett at 200 Crescent Court, Suite 1080, Dallas, Texas 75201 or call (214) 855-8999 or (800) 992-5922.

Bobbie Probstein is a writer and photographer whose new book, *Healing Now*, has been widely praised. It is invaluable for anyone affected by illness or preparing for surgery. Her first book, an autobiography, Return to Center, is in its third printing. She may be reached at P.O. Box 3654, Dana Point, California 92629-8654.

Bob Proctor is the President of Bob Proctor Seminars and the founder of the Million Dollar Forum in Ontario, Canada. Bob is the author of *You Were Born Rich* and conducts Born Rich Seminars all over the world. Bob's seminars empower people to create the life they've always dreamed about. You can contact him at Million Dollar International, 211 Consumers Road, Suite 201, Willowdale, Ontario, Canada M2J 4G8 or call (416) 498-6700.

Nido Qubein, C.S.P., C.P.A.E., is past president of the National Speakers Association and is an outstanding speaker on sales, management and marketing. His many books include *Get The Best From Yourself, Communicate Like A Pro* and *Professional Selling Techniques*. He can be reached at Creative Services, Inc., P.O. Box 6008, High Point, North Carolina 27262-6008 or call (919) 889-3010.

Anthony Robbins, nationally recognized as the leader in the field of human-development training, is the author of two best-sellers, *Unlimited Power* and *Awaken the Giant Within: How to Take Immediate Control of Your Mental, Emotional, Physical and Financial Destiny!* During the past decade more than a million people have invested in and benefited from his seminars, audiotapes, videotapes and books. He is the founder of nine companies, a consultant to businesses and governments in the U.S. and abroad, and a committed philanthropist with the creation of The Anthony Robbins Foundation. For more information on products and services, call Robbins Research International, Inc. at 1-800-

445-8183 or write the company at 9191 Towne Centre Drive, Suite 600, San Diego, California 92122.

Pamela Rogers earned her Masters Degree in Education from The University of Pennsylvania in 1990 and teaches second grade at Reynolds Elementary School in Philadelphia. She studies acting when she's not teaching.

Glenna Salsbury, C.S.P., C.P.A.E., graduated from Northwestern University in Evanston, Illinois, obtained her Masters Degree from UCLA and, 16 years later, earned a Masters of Theology from Fuller Seminary. In 1980 Glenna founded her own company which provides keynote presentations and personal growth seminars. In her personal life, Glenna is married to Jim Salsbury, a former Detroit Lion and Green Bay Packer and has three daughters. Call or write to obtain her powerful six-pack tape album entitled, *Passion, Power and Purpose.* She can be reached at 9228 North 64th Place, Paradise Valley, Arizona 85253 or call (602) 483-7732.

Jack Schlatter, a former teacher, is currently a motivational speaker. He can be reached at P.O. Box 577, Cypress, California 90630 or call (714) 879-7271.

Lee Shapiro is a former trial attorney and judge who left law practice because he never received a standing ovation from a jury! He is now a speaker and professor specializing in ethics in management, keynote addresses and people skills. He can be reached at 5700-12 Baltimore Drive, La Mesa, California 91942 or (619) 668-9036.

Frank Siccone, Ed.D., is the director of the Siccone Institute in San Francisco. He is a consultant to numerous schools and businesses. His books include *Responsibility: The Most Basic R and 101 Ways To Develop Student Self-Esteem And Responsibility* with Jack Canfield (Allyn & Bacon). He can be reached at the Siccone Institute, 2151 Union Street, San Francisco, California 94123 or call (415) 922-2244.

Cindy Spitzer is a free-lance writer who helped us rewrite several of our most difficult and important stories. She can be reached at 5027 Berwyn Road, College Park, Maryland 20740.

Jeffrey Michael Thomas is a regional vice-president for Van Kampen Merritt, a professional money management firm. He is a member of the National Speakers Association and speaks on topics ranging from financial management to fund-raising for various charities through his company, J. Michael Thomas & Associates. Mr. Thomas lives and works in Tustin, California, and he is currently seeking a seat on the Tustin City Council. He can be reached at (714) 544-1352.

Pamela Truax is the author of *Small Business Pitfalls And Bridges.* She can be reached at 2073 Columbia Way, Vista, California 92083 or call (619) 598-6008.

Francis Xavier Trujillo, Ed.D., is Founder and President of *ProTeach Publications,* a firm specializing in the creation and production of inspirational and esteem-building posters, cards and related materials for students and teachers. His writings, primarily in poster format, are found gracing the walls of virtually every school in the United States. Titles include *Who Builds the Builders?, The Power to Teach, A Letter to My Students* and *Giver of A Lifelong Gift.* Frank speaks on a variety of issues related to self-esteem, teacher empowerment and education reform. He can be reached at *ProTeach Publications,* P.O. Box 19262, Sacramento, CA 95819 (800) 233-3541. Write or call for his full-color catalog depicting *Bilding Me A Fewchr* and dozens of other posters and related inspirational materials. *Bilding Me A Fewchr* became the basis for the *Build Me A Future Project,* a nationwide, non-partisan, letter-writing campaign wherein kids of all ages sent letters to President Clinton suggesting ways in which we can work together to help build us all a better future.

Dottie Walters is President of the Walters International Speakers Bureau in California. She sends paid speakers all over the world and is heavily involved in presentation training. She is the author, with her daughter Lilly, of the new Simon and Schuster book, *Speak And Grow Rich,* and is founder and administrator of the International Group of Agents and Bureaus. Dottie publishes *Sharing Ideas,* the largest news magazine in the world for paid professional speakers. You can write her at P.O. Box 1120, Glendora, California 91740 or call (818) 335-8069 or fax (818) 335-6127.

Bettie Youngs is President of Instruction & Professional Development, Inc., a resource and consulting firm providing in-service to school districts. Bettie is a former Iowa Teacher-of-the-Year, is currently Professor at San Diego State University and

Executive Director of the Phoenix Foundation. She is the author of 14 books including *The Educator's Self-Esteem: It's Criteria #1, The 6 Vital Ingredients Of Self-Esteem And How To Develop Them In Students* and *Safeguarding Your Teenager From The Dragons Of Life.* She can be reached at 3060 Racetrack View Drive, Del Mar, California 92014 or call (619) 481-6360.

Acknowledgments *(continued)*

The Royal Knights Of Harlem from *Revolution From Within: A Book of Self-Esteem* by Gloria Steinem. Reprinted by permission of Little, Brown & Company. ©1992 Gloria Steinem.

Willing To Pay The Price from *Self Made in America* by John McCormack. Reprinted by permission of Addison-Wesley Publishing Co., Inc., and the author. ©1990 by The Visible Changes Educational Foundation and David R. Legge.

The Power Of Optimism. Excerpts from *The Power of Optimism* by Alan Loy McGinnis. ©1990 by Alan Loy McGinnis. Reprinted by permission of HarperCollins Publishers.

Two Monks from *Wisdom of the Zen Masters* by Irmgard Schloegl. Reprinted with permission of New Directions Publishing Corporation. ©1975 Irmgard Schloegl.

Love: The One Creative Force. Reprinted by permission of Eric Butterworth. ©1992 Eric Butterworth.

All I Remember and *The Bag Lady.* Reprinted by permission of Bobbie Probstein. ©1992 Bobbie Probstein.

Heart Songs. Reprinted by permission of Patricia Jean Hansen. ©1992 Patricia Jean Hansen.

True Love. Reprinted by permission of Barry Vissell. ©1992 Barry Vissell.

It Can't Happen Here. Reprinted by permission of Pamela Rogers. ©1992 Pamela Rogers.

Who You Are Makes a Difference. Reprinted by permission of Helice Bridges. ©1992 Helice Bridges.

A Brother Like That. Reprinted by permission of Dan Clark. ©1992 Dan Clark.

Big Ed. Reprinted by permission of Joe Batten. ©1989 by AMACOM Books.

Love And The Cabbie. Reprinted by permission of Art Buchwald. ©1992 Art Buchwald.

A Simple Gesture and *I Am a Teacher.* Reprinted with permission of John Wayne Schlatter. ©1992 John Schlatter.

The Smile, Did The Earth Move For You and *Just One More Time.* Reprinted by permission of Dr. Hanoch McCarty. ©1991 Hanoch McCarty and Associates.

A Story For Valentine's Day. Reprinted by permission of Jo Ann Larsen. ©1992 Jo Ann Larsen.

Carpe Diem! from *Dare to Be Yourself* by Alan Cohen. Reprinted by permission of Alan Cohen. ©1991 Alan Cohen Publications. For a free catalog of Alan Cohen's books, tapes, and workshop schedule, write to P.O. Box 98509, Des Moines, WA 98198, or call (800) 462-3013.

I Know You, You're Just Like Me. Reprinted by permission of the Human Awareness Institute. ©1992 Stan V. Dale.

Puppies for Sale. Reprinted by permission of Dan Clark. ©1989 Dan Clark.

Nothing But The Truth! Reprinted by permission of David Casstevens.

Children Learn What They Live. Reprinted by permission of Dorothy Law Nolte.

Touched. Used by permission of Victor H. Nelson. ©1990 Victor H. Nelson. This article first appeared in the May/June 1990 issue of the *Family Therapy Networker.*

I Love You, Son! by Victor Brook Miller. Used by permission of The Institute for Humanistic and Transpersonal Education. ©1977 IHTE.

What You Are Is As Important As What You Do. Reprinted by permission of Patricia Fripp. ©1992 Patricia Fripp.

The Perfect American Family. Reprinted by permission of Michael Murphy, Ed.D. ©1992 Michael Murphy Ed.D.

Just Say It! Reprinted by permission of Gene Bedley. ©1992 Gene Bedley.

A Legacy Of Love. Reprinted by permission of Bobbie Gee. ©1992 Bobbie Gee.

I Like Myself Now from *Man, The Manipulator* by Everett L. Shostrom. Used by permission. ©1967 Abingdon Press.

All The Good Things. Reprinted by permission of Helen P. Mrosla. OSF, and Shippensburg University ©1991 Shippensburg University. This article originally appeared in *Proteus: A Journal of Ideas,* Spring 1991. Reprinted with permission from the October, 1991 *Readers Digest.*

The Little Boy by Helen E. Buckley. Reprinted by permission from "Glad To Be Me — Building Self-Esteem in Yourself and Others." ©1989 Dov Peretz Elkins. (Princeton, NJ: Growth Associates).

I Think I Can! Reprinted by permission of Michele Borba. ©1992 Michele Borba.

Rest In Peace: The "I Can't" Funeral. Reprinted by permission of Chick Moorman. ©1992 Chick Moorman.

The 333 Story. Reprinted with permission of Robert C. Proctor. ©1992 Robert Proctor.

There Are No Vans! Reprinted by permission of Anthony Robbins.

If You Don't Ask, You Don't Get — But If You Do, You Do. Reprinted by permission of Rick Gelinas. ©1992 Rick Gelinas.

The Magic Of Believing. Reprinted by permission of Dale Madden, President of Island Heritage Publishing, a division of The Madden Corporation. ©1992 Dale Madden.

Glenna's Goal Book. Reprinted by permission of Glenna Salsbury. ©1991 Salsbury Enterprises.

Another Check Mark On The List. Reprinted by permission of John Goddard. ©1992 John Goddard.

The Box and *You've Got Yourself A Deal.* Reprinted by permission of Florence Littauer. ©1992 Florence Littauer, President, CLASS Speakers, Inc., Author of 20 books including: *Silver Boxes, Dare to Dream* and *Personality Plus.*

Encouragement. Reprinted with permission of Nido R. Qubein. ©1992 Nido R. Qubein.

Try Something Different. Reprinted with permission of Price Pritchett, Ph.D. ©1990 Price Pritchett, Ph.D.

Service With A Smile from *Service America,* page 128. Reprinted by permission of Dow Jones/Irwin. ©1985 Karl Albrecht & Ron Zenke.

Obstacles. Reprinted by permission of Beacon Press. ©1992 Viktor E. Frankl.

John Corcoran — The Man Who Couldn't Read. Reprinted by permission of John Corcoran. ©1992 John Corcoran.

Don't Be Afraid To Fail ©1981 United Technologies Corporation, Hartford, CT 06101.

The Ultimate Rebounder. Reprinted by permission of Danielle Kennedy. ©1991 Danielle Kennedy/Prentice Hall.

Failure? No! — Just Temporary Setbacks. Reprinted by permission of Dorothy Walters. ©1992 Dorothy Walters.

For Me To Be More Creative, I Am Waiting For . . . Reprinted by permission of the Center for Creative Leadership, Greensboro, NC ©1992 , *Issues and Observations.* The center is a non-profit educational institute working to adapt the theories and ideas of the behavioral sciences to the practical concerns of managers and leaders. To receive information about the Center's work, or a free subscription to *Issues and Observations,* please write: Center for Creative Leadership, P.O. Box 26300, Greensboro, NC 27438-6300 or call (919) 288-7210.

The Power Of Determination. Reprinted by permission of Burt Dubin. ©1992 Burt Dubin.

She Saved 219 Lives. Reprinted by permission of Betty Tisdale. ©1992 Betty Tisdale.

There Is Greatness All Around You — Use It! Reprinted with permission of Bob Richards. ©1992 Bob Richards.

Take A Moment To Really See! Reprinted with permission of Jeffrey M. Thomas. ©1992 Jeffrey M. Thomas.

If I Had To Live My Life Over by Nadine Stair. This poem, which has been passed around and reprinted for years, has been attributed to Nadine Stair. It was supposedly written at age 85. The general consensus is that she was living in the state of Kentucky at the time she wrote the poem. We have been unable to contact any family to verify these claims.

The Dolphin's Gift. Excerpted from *The Dolphin's Gift* ©1980. Reprinted with permission of New World Library, San Rafael, CA 94903.

Jack Canfield is the President of Self-Esteem Seminars and The Canfield Training Group, a seminar and training company dedicated to assisting individuals and organizations to live in alignment with their highest purpose and aspirations. Jack conducts in-house trainings for corporations, government agencies and school districts and public seminars for individuals. He also delivers keynote speeches for state regional and national conferences and conventions.

The following workshops, seminars and consulting services are available from The Canfield Training Group:

Self-Esteem And Peak Performance

Self-Esteem: The Bottom Line To Success

Self-Esteem: Learning To Love And Express Yourself

Self-Esteem In The Classroom: A Workshop For Teachers And Counselors

How To Build High Self-Esteem

Parenting For High Self-Esteem

The Ten Steps To Success

Visionary Selling: How To Become A World Class Salesperson

The Couples Seminar: How To Have An Affair With Your Spouse

The Self-Esteem Facilitating Skills Seminar: Training The Trainers

The STAR Program: A Video-Based Corporate Training Program

The GOALS Program: A Video-Based Training For At-Risk Adults

Jack also has a wide variety of books, audio cassette and video cassette programs available. If you would like to receive a brochure or discuss a possible workshop or speaking date, please contact him by calling (310) 337-9222 or 1-800-2-ESTEEM.

Mark Victor Hansen's clients call him "America's Business Motivator." Fortune 500 companies and their professional associations have been engaging Mark for over 18 years to share his vast talents and resources in the areas of sales excellence and strategies, and personal empowerment and development.

Mark has spent a lifetime dedicated to his mission to make a profound and positive difference in peoples' lives. Each year people experience Mark all over the world as he travels over 250,000 miles internationally and speaks more than 200 times annually. Throughout his career, he has inspired hundreds of thousands of people to create for themselves a more powerful, purposeful future while stimulating the sale of millions of dollars worth of goods and services.

His book *Future Diary* is read by thousands across the country. *Dare To Win,* his latest book, has been highly endorsed by Norman Vincent Peale and Og Mandino, both legends in the area of personal development. In addition, he has written *How To Achieve Total Prosperity* and the *Miracle Of Tithing,* all best-sellers.

As well as speaking and writing, Mark has produced a complete library of personal empowerment cassette and video programs that have enabled his listeners to recognize and use their innate abilities in their business and personal lives. His message has also made him a popular television and radio personality. "The Mark Victor Hansen Show" aired in Southern California on HBO, as well as a pilot for PBS entitled "Build A Better You." *Success Magazine* reported his achievement on the cover of their August 1991 issue.

Mark is a big man with a big heart and a big spirit, an inspiration to all who seek to better themselves.

You can contact Mark by calling (714) 759-9304 or from outside of California (800) 433-2314.